LONDON'S MARKETS

LONDON'S MARKETS

FROM SMITHFIELD TO PORTOBELLO ROAD

STEPHEN HALLIDAY

First published 2014

The History Press
The Mill, Brimscombe Port
Stroud, Gloucestershire, GL5 2QG
www.thehistorypress.co.uk

British Library Cataloguing in Publication Data.
A catalogue record for this book is available from the British Library.

ISBN 978 0 7524 9448 7

Typesetting and origination by The History Press
Printed in Great Britain

Contents

Introduction:
The City of Markets

London is a city of markets. It always has been. The earliest was in the Roman Forum, dating from AD 70. It was part of a civic centre that included arcades to shelter market traders and customers from the inclement Londinium weather. The foot of one of the supporting columns may still be seen in the basement of hairdressers' Nicholson and Griffin at No. 90, Gracechurch Street, close to the site of Leadenhall Market that lies at the heart of the Roman city. One of the oldest place names in London is Aldwych. It means 'old market place' and was granted to the defeated Danes by Alfred the Great as a place where they could trade on the fringe of the City of London. Mediaeval London contained hundreds of markets selling everything from meat, fish, fruit, vegetables and cheese to clothing, precious metals, religious artefacts and timber. Many of today's street names remind the observant pedestrian of the markets that were to be found in them in the time of Richard Whittington: Bread Street, Milk Street and Ironmonger Lane are still visible but some have disappeared such as Fish Street off the present Knightrider Street. Some of London's markets have also disappeared. John Stow, in his *Survey of London* written in 1598, tells his readers of 'Cornhill Ward, so called of a corn market, time out of mind there holden' though he informs us that it was also a market for 'old apparel', presumably second-hand clothing.

John Stow (1524–1605)

Stow was born in Cornhill, the son of a prosperous tallow chandler. Although there is no record of his education at school or university he became a collector of manuscripts, particularly on the history and customs of London, and a fluent writer. He was at one time suspected of Catholic sympathies but never prosecuted and he gained the support of such influential courtiers as the Earl of Leicester and

Archbishops Whitgift and Parker, the latter himself a collector of ancient manuscripts. Stow became a member of the Merchant Taylors Livery Company and his *Survey of London*, published first in 1598, is a definitive account of events, customs and personalities in London in the late sixteenth century and remains in print. His tomb in the City church of St Andrew Undershaft, off Leadenhall Street, has a striking monument to him, quill pen in hand.

Cornhill was also the site of a famous pillory that was primarily used for dealers in sub-standard goods, though it was once occupied by the author of *Robinson Crusoe*, Daniel Defoe, for writing a satirical work, *The Shortest Way with Dissenters*, which offended the government. Samuel Pepys's *Diary* contains many references to the pleasures he derived from 'marketing' (or as we would say 'shopping') and many of the markets he used, like Leadenhall and Smithfield, may be visited today. The Port of London, which for centuries was the world's largest, was itself a huge market for produce from throughout the world. In the Tudor era London started to become a major centre for financial markets such as insurance, currency trading and investment funds. It remains one of the world's leading financial markets. In the reign of Victoria antiques

The Aldwych, whose grand buildings now occupy the site of a market granted to the Danes by Alfred the Great. (Wikimedia Commons, gohsuket)

markets began to emerge, one of the world's largest, at Portobello Road, starting to trade at that time. Markets, from conventional food and clothes markets to those that specialise in the sale of stolen valuables ('hot gear'), have flourished throughout London's history; they are the reason for London's existence and continuing prosperity.

Ronnie, Reggie and George

Many of these ancient markets still prosper in new locations. Covent Garden remains a market though the fruit and vegetable wholesale market which it formerly accommodated has moved to Lambeth. Billingsgate's fish market, which began to trade in mediaeval London, moved to a site in the shadow of Canary Wharf in 1982. The former market building still exists, a fine example of Victorian civic design by the architect of Smithfield Market and Tower Bridge, Sir Horace Jones. It once provided employment for such diverse characters as the writer George Orwell and the infamous Kray twins, Ronnie and Reggie, and the building is now used for city conferences and musical events. Other markets with long histories have survived on or close to their original sites: Smithfield, Lloyd's, Borough Market (which predates William the Conqueror) and Petticoat Lane are examples. Some historic markets have seen their sites occupied by new users. The former site of the Baltic Exchange, destroyed by a Provisional IRA bomb in 1992, is now occupied by the City's celebrated Gherkin, itself a trading centre for financial markets. The Baltic Exchange has moved to a new home next to the Gherkin. The Victorian halls of Spitalfields Market, which originated in the thirteenth century as a market for fruit and vegetables, now accommodate sellers of fashion, art and antiques.

Each of the markets described in the pages which follow has a long, fascinating and often controversial history and most still exist though fires, wars and developments in fashion and technology have often wrought changes which would make them unrecognisable to their original occupants. A short section is devoted to markets which have disappeared though in some cases they are remembered by street and place names. Most of the markets mentioned here can be seen and visited though in some cases visiting times are restricted and in others the advent of computerised trading means that their activities are in the land of virtual reality where they may not be glimpsed. Details of times for visiting are included where relevant though it is wise to check them via their websites since they do change. Many offer real bargains to a discerning buyer so, like Samuel Pepys, start 'marketing' now!

In writing this account of London's markets I have been assisted by many people but two of them I single out for services beyond the call of duty. My friends Peter Clark and Martyn Webb, who between them have over eighty years' experience of London's stock market and Lloyd's insurance market respectively, were kind enough to read the drafts of those two chapters and correct a number of errors. I am in their debt. Any errors that remain are my own.

1

Smithfield: London's Meat Market

In the Middle Ages the expanse of grass beyond the city walls was known as the 'Smooth Field' and its use for grazing cattle and sheep made it a suitable location for the City's livestock market, which existed a century before the Norman conquest. Some local street names like Cow Cross Street derive from this use while others, like Cock Lane, tell us that poultry was sold there. In 1123 some nearby land was granted to King Henry I's jester, Rahere, for the site of the Priory and Hospital of St Bartholomew, London's oldest, which benefited from the right to hold a weekly fair selling cloth: hence the nearby street name Cloth Fair. In 1133 the right was granted to hold an annual Bartholomew Fair beginning on St Bartholomew's day, 24 August and continuing for four days. So celebrated, and eventually notorious, was this event that Ben Johnson wrote a play called *Bartholomew Fair* in 1613. The City authorities finally suppressed the fair more than seven centuries later, in 1855, because of the mounting crime, mayhem and debauchery that accompanied it. In 1174 the chronicler William Fitzstephen had recorded the 'smooth field where every Friday there is a celebrated rendezvous of fine horses to be sold and in another quarter are placed vendibles of the peasant, swine with their deep flanks and cows and oxen of immense bulk'. By the time of John Stow in the late sixteenth century, Smithfield had become associated with the sale and racing of horses, 'strong steeds, well limbed geldings whom the buyers do especially regard for pace and swiftness; the boys which ride these horses, sometimes two, sometimes three, do run races for wagers …' The first recorded race meeting in England took place at Smithfield in 1174, in the reign of Henry II, and, a few years after Stow wrote his account, James I introduced horse racing to Newmarket, where it remains. In *Henry IV Part II*, Shakespeare has Falstaff say of Bardolph, 'He'll buy me a horse in Smithfield'. Stow went on to explain that, in addition to horses, 'fat swine, milch kine (dairy cows) sheep and oxen' were also being sold at Smithfield.

Martyrs, Fire, Gluttony and a Scottish Hero

In the meantime the Smooth Field had acquired a more sinister reputation as London's principal site for the execution of criminals and dissidents. Protestant martyrs were burned at the stake, forgers were boiled alive and a plaque marks the spot where the Scottish hero William Wallace was executed in 1305. In 1381 the Peasants' Revolt reached its bloody climax here when the Lord Mayor, William Walworth, stabbed its leader, Wat Tyler. In 1666 it marked the north-western boundary of the Great Fire that had consumed the City, the conflagration finally burning itself out at Pye Corner at the junction of Cock Lane and Giltspur Street, the event being still marked here by a small statue of the Golden Boy of Pye Corner. An inscription beneath the statue attributed the fire to 'the sin of gluttony', a reference to the meat pies and other produce consumed at the market.

Bulls in a China Shop

Amidst all this the livestock market continued to prosper. John Carpenter's *Liber Albus* in his section on 'Customs of Smithfield' recorded that it cost one (old) penny to sell a cow or ox there and the same fee for twelve sheep. Moreover 'foreign dealers' (by which he meant merchants from beyond Middlesex) trading between St Martin's day (11 November) and Christmas had to give their 'third best beast' to the market bailiff in return for trading there. Presumably this reflected the fact that 'foreign' merchants came from outside the capital to take advantage of the Christmas trade. Carpenter also recorded that freemen of the City had the right to show beasts for sale at Smithfield free of charge.

The *Liber Albus*

Also known as the 'White Book', the *Liber Albus* was compiled in 1419 by John Carpenter, clerk to the City of London, during the last mayoralty of Richard Whittington (*c.* 1354–1423) and is a detailed record of the customs, regulations and privileges of the City, gathered from records going back to the years before the Norman Conquest, many of the records now lost. It is an invaluable source of information on London during the mediaeval period, with detailed accounts of its commerce, taxes and penalties for such misdemeanours as selling bad fish or loaves deficient in weight or quality.

Old Smithfield Market, 1824. (Wikimedia Commons, Jacques-Laurent Agasse)

As London grew, so did the market, which by the late eighteenth century was no longer an isolated pasture but increasingly surrounded by shops and dwellings. In 1710 a wooden fence was built to contain the livestock and prevent them from encroaching on nearby streets and other markets like Cloth Fair whose entrance, on market days, was protected by a chain. By the 1840s over two hundred thousand cattle and one and a half million sheep were annually, in the words of a contemporary *Farmer's Magazine*, being, 'violently forced into an area of five acres, in the very heart of London, through its narrowest and most crowded thoroughfares'. The Lord Mayor complained about the multitude of 'loose, idle and disorderly persons' that the market attracted and the situation was not helped by drovers who amused themselves by goading the terrified animals into a state of panic in the hope that they would run amok and destroy neighbouring properties, giving rise to the phrase 'bull in a china shop'. There were also cases of 'wife-selling' of the kind that began Thomas Hardy's *The Mayor of Casterbridge*.

'Horrid abominations'

For Londoners in the mid-1800s the existence of the live cattle market had become a source of concern on the grounds of public health. One writer complained in 1843 that, 'Of all the horrid abominations with which London has been cursed there is not one that can come up to that disgusting place West Smithfield in the very heart of the most Christian and polished City in the world' while at the same time the poet Thomas Hood penned an *Ode to the Advocates for the Removal of Smithfield Market*. In *Oliver Twist*, published in 1838, Charles Dickens described Smithfield as 'Ankle deep in filth and mire, a thick steam perpetually arising from the bodies of the cattle' and surrounded by 'unwashed, unshaven, squalid and dirty figures'. He continued to condemn the market, writing in 1851 that, 'A beast market in the heart of Paris would be regarded an impossible nuisance … One of these benighted frog-eaters would scarcely understand your meaning if you told him of the existence of such a British bulwark'. In response to such complaints Parliament, in 1852, authorised the construction of a live cattle market at Copenhagen Fields, Islington, to the north of King's Cross in an area which at that time (though not for much longer) was still rural. The new market was opened in 1855 by Prince Albert, clearing the way for the former market at Smithfield to be redeveloped.

The New Market: Floating Runways

Construction of the present Smithfield meat market on the site of the old livestock market took two years (1866–68) and was undertaken to the designs of the City architect (later Sir) Horace Jones (1819–87) who was also responsible for Billingsgate Market, Leadenhall Market and Tower Bridge. It cost almost a million pounds, a huge sum for the time, and consisted of two wings known as East Market and West Market separated by the Grand Avenue. These are all Grade II listed buildings today. The market had its own railway station in a tunnel beneath the market that could be reached from King's Cross and Blackfriars stations. The station no longer operates but the former railway sidings have become a car park and the tunnel is used by Thameslink services whose passengers are quite unaware of their proximity to the famous market. A lavish opening ceremony on 24 November 1868 was performed by the Lord Mayor, accompanied by the band of the Grenadier Guards and followed by a banquet. The market was later extended to accommodate poultry and fish and installed one of the capital's first cold stores, following the arrival of refrigerated meat from Australia and New Zealand. The first consignment arrived on 2 February 1880. The market now covers 10 acres: about twice the area of the former livestock market. In the Second World War the Nobel Prize-winning scientist Max Perutz used one of Smithfield's cold stores in an attempt to allow the refuelling of aeroplanes protecting the shipping lanes against U-boats. He experimented with the development of a material suitable for building floating runways to be positioned in the mid-Atlantic but in vain. The RAF decided that they preferred long-distance planes!

Grand Avenue, Smithfield, by Sir Horace Jones. (Oxyman)

The End of Rationing

Unlike the other wholesale markets such as Covent Garden, which have moved from the City centre to more accessible and spacious premises further away, Smithfield has developed and prospered on the site that has been London's source of meat for 1,000 years. On 4 July 1954, Smithfield was the scene of a celebration that marked the end of the rationing that began in 1940, early in the Second World War. On that day, meat, the last item to be rationed, became freely available for the first time in fourteen years. Smithfield opened at midnight to mark the event and ration books were ceremonially burned. The buildings were substantially refurbished by the City Corporation in 1992 and parts of the site have been, and remain, objects of controversy as proposals to demolish and redevelop some buildings are regularly put forward and usually refused after lengthy enquiries. Watch this space.

'Antique working practices'

The market is busy from 9 p.m. unloading the vehicles that bring the fresh meat for the following day's trading. 'Shunters' move lorries into bays for unloading where 'pullers-back', working within the vehicles, move the meat from the front to the back of the vehicle from which 'pitchers' unload it and take it to the stalls. There it is dismembered by 'cutters', weighed by 'scales-men' and sometimes moved from stall to stall by 'humpers' or on the trolleys of 'bummarees'. 'Deliverymen' take the meat to the customers' vehicles while 'offal boys', young apprentices, look on to learn their trades as their fathers and uncles work. In 1969 a report on the operations of the market described it as, 'a picture of antique working practices' and the epitome of the 'pre-entry closed shop' whereby all vacancies were filled at 8 a.m. on Tuesdays by the Transport and General Workers' Union. Any stallholder who employed his own labour would be boycotted by 'pitchers' and receive no meat at his stall! When questioned by a researcher about the reasons for these practices a union official replied, with disarming honesty, 'Self-interest, the same as barristers and solicitors'! Because of its long and unsocial hours the Smithfield area is particularly well supplied with pubs and restaurants which serve excellent food and drink at all times to the market's workers who are noted connois-seurs of good fare.

Smithfield Market, 2010. (Jorge Royan)

When Can I Visit?

Trading at Smithfield begins at 3 a.m. and ends at noon, Monday to Friday, though many stalls cease to trade at 7 a.m. by which time the retailers, cater-ing contractors, hoteliers and restaurateurs have made their purchases and departed. Anyone, including visitors, can buy produce from the stalls and in the week before Christmas many private individuals travel to Smithfield to purchase their poultry, game and hams as their mediaeval ancestors did. It is also possible to walk around the markets after midday when they are very quiet. For those who wish to learn more about how the market operates City of London blue badge guides conduct walking tours of the market beginning at 7 a.m. and lasting an hour and a half. The guide will tell you of the activities of the assortment of oddly-named and carefully demarcated trades which handle 150,000 tons of meat each year, the jobs often being passed from father to son. Booking for the tours is essential and may be made at info@ cityoflondontouristguides.com. The tour takes ninety minutes and costs £8 (£6 concessions). The market is the starting point for a cycle race called the Smithfield Nocturne featuring professional as well as amateur cyclists racing around London at night. The event has its own website which gives details: www.londonnocturne.com.

Places of Interest Nearby

The nearby church of St Bartholomew-the-Great, founded in 1123, survived the Great Fire and contains the ornate tomb of the founder of the hospital and priory, Rahere. It once contained a printing works that employed Benjamin Franklin. The almost equally ancient church of St Bartholomew-the-Less is

nearby, and is of an unusual octagonal shape, its parish consisting simply of the hospital. Reference has previously been made to the monument to William Wallace, which was set into the wall of St Bartholomew's Hospital in 1956. Number 43, Cloth Fair is the former home of the poet laureate Sir John Betjeman whose residence there is marked by a blue plaque. The building now belongs to the Landmark Trust and it is possible to stay there.

The former home of poet Sir John Betjeman at No. 43 Cloth Fair, adjacent to Smithfield, is marked by a blue plaque. (Wikimedia Commons, public domain)

2

From Copenhagen to Bermondsey: New Caledonian Market and 'hot gear'

Smithfield livestock market closed, to the relief of its neighbours, on 11 June 1855 and the new Metropolitan Cattle Market was opened by Prince Albert two days later in Copenhagen Fields, north of King's Cross Station and close to the station's goods yards to which live sheep and cattle were brought. A slaughter house was also built on the site. The new market was built by the City Corporation on the former site of Copenhagen House, a property constructed in the early years of the seventeenth century to accommodate the entourage of the Danish king when he was visiting his brother-in-law King James I. The Corporation bought the 74-acre site in 1852 and spent three years clearing it and building pens to hold the livestock that was to be driven there from the goods yard. The pens, which could hold 40,000 animals, were surrounded by iron railings surmounted by figures representing the animals traded there. Many of the railings remain though these figures have been removed. They did not always restrain the animals as planned and there were several cases of bulls escaping, as at Smithfield. On one occasion a bull was cornered, appropriately, in front of a sign advertising Bovril. Several pubs were built to accommodate market traders of which most, including The Butcher's Arms may still be seen. A clock tower was built as the central feature of the market to a design by the City architect J.B. Bunning. It is still a prominent feature of the area, which is now mostly occupied by dwellings.

Cloth Fair Revived

By the time that the livestock market moved from Smithfield the former Cloth Fair had developed into a market selling much more than cloth. It had, in effect, become a market for general merchandise whose stallholders, denied the large numbers of visitors associated with the former livestock market,

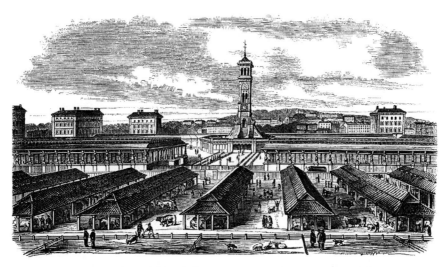

Newly opened Metropolitan Cattle Market, 1855.

sought another home. The costermongers ('barrow boys') who had lost their Smithfield audience, along with refugees from the recently (1855) proscribed Bartholomew Fair, approached the City Corporation to ask that on Fridays, when the new Metropolitan Cattle Market did not trade, they could be admitted to the new market 'according to ancient custom, among the empty cattle pens'. The Corporation, no doubt attracted by the prospect of renting out empty space on an extra day a week, agreed to the request and within a few weeks the Caledonian Market was born, taking its name from the nearby Caledonian Road.

Prince Monolulu and 'dark beads'

Within a few months the Caledonian Market had become an established feature of London's commercial life. The gates would open at 10 a.m. on Fridays to admit 'runners', young men noted for their speed and athleticism, who would be despatched by stallholders to occupy the most favourable pitches and register their claim with the Clerk of the Market who was responsible for collecting rents. Amongst the more exotic attractions were Prince Monolulu, a huge Ethiopian who offered to sell racing tips with the cry 'I gotta horse, I gotta horse' and the banana king who, besides bananas, sold 'peaches like a maiden's cheek'. Honey Jelly Pills, 'To purify the blood', were amongst many quack remedies on sale. However, genuine bargains were also to be had. On 19 January 1932 the *Morning Post* carried an account of a young woman who had bought a necklace of 'dark beads', for the price of 7*s* 6*d*, which were soon recognised as black pearls and sold for £20,000. More prosaically, shortly afterwards a first edition of *Alice in Wonderland* was bought for one old penny and sold for £10. In 1916 a Wounded Allies Great War Fair raised £30,000 for wounded soldiers.

Silver Kings and Stolen Goods

The market became especially well known as an outlet for silver and for stall-holders known as Caledonian Silver Kings, much of their merchandise having been acquired through theft. The market enjoyed the status of a marché ouvert (open market), a concept dating from mediaeval times under which stolen goods sold in certain markets between sunrise and sunset became the legal property of the purchaser. It originated at a time when people did not travel far so, if the owner of property that had been stolen failed to search for them in his local market (where they were most likely to be for sale) between sunrise and sunset on market day he lost title to them.

Film Stars, Royalty and Americans

By the 1930s the sale of livestock had declined as Smithfield's ready-slaugh-tered meat took over the market but over 2,000 stalls were regularly to be found in the Friday market and it was attracting celebrity visitors, including the film star Greta Garbo and the Prince of Wales soon, briefly, to be King Edward VIII. In 1932 the popular novelist J.B. Priestley wrote an account of the market that emphasised its enduring popularity with American visitors:

> You may pay ten shillings more for a silver bowl or an amber necklace in the Caledonian Market than you would pay in a decent shop in the centre of the city but you are being given more than ten shillings worth of roman-tic legend with the articles. The story of how you picked them up will be worth a whole heap of dollars to you, once back in the home town.

The fascination for Americans remained long after the market had moved. In the 1980s a former habitué of the market, Fred White, encountered two Texans, complete with Stetsons, at Caledonian Road Station looking for the cattle market. The closest underground stations to the former site, with its prominent clock tower and surviving railings, are King's Cross and Angel.

New Caledonia

During the Second World War the market was closed and the site was used as a lorry park for vehicles belonging to the army and to the Royal Mail.

Caledonian Park Clock Tower, 2005. (Gordon Joly)

The cattle market never reopened but when the war ended a petition, signed by 13,500 stallholders and customers, requested that the Friday market be restored. The original site had been designated for housing, only the clock tower remaining of the original buildings. In 1950 the market was reopened as the New Caledonian Market at Bermondsey Square in Southwark on the former site of Bermondsey Abbey, the opening ceremony being performed by the actress Valerie Hobson, later the wife of John Profumo, MP and cabinet minister. The *marché ouvert* status accompanied the market to its new site where 'hot gear' continued to be traded. The concept was abolished in 1995 though old habits die hard and customers arriving early may still find valuable objects being discreetly offered from the backs of vans for payment in cash. The market is now mostly devoted to antiques, along with jewellery, paintings, clocks, ceramics and glass. It is also referred to as Bermondsey Market and continues to be popular with foreign visitors, especially Americans, as J.B. Priestley noted of its predecessor.

WHEN CAN I VISIT?

The market is open every Friday from 4 a.m., with trading from 5 a.m. (though alert visitors may find some sales being made from the backs of vans before that time) and ends at about midday. The closest underground station is Borough.

PLACES OF INTEREST NEARBY

The area close to the market has many associations with Charles Dickens. Lant Street, near Borough Station, was the home both of Dickens and of David Copperfield with Dickens's characters being commemorated in Little Dorrit Court, Trundle Street, Weller Street and Copperfield Street. The church of St George the Martyr, next to the station, has a Little Dorrit East Window to mark where Little Dorrit married Arthur Clennam. Also nearby, just off Borough High Street, is Angel Place where a wall plaque marks a remaining fragment of the Marshalsea debtors' prison to which Dickens's father and several of Dickens's characters were committed. Chaucer's Tabard Inn was demolished in 1873 but its former site is commemorated by a blue plaque in Talbot Yard, off Borough High Street close to its junction with Southwark Street. The neighbouring George Inn, owned by the National Trust, is London's oldest coaching inn. Look out too for Leathermarket Street, which was the home of the Leather, Hide and Wool Exchange, now a building devoted to residences, small workshops and a smart restaurant. It is a reminder of the fact that, in the eighteenth and nineteenth centuries, Bermondsey grew up as the centre of the British trade in tanning leather. Hides were bought from London butchers, water and oak bark for the tanning process were available from the river Ravensbourne and from Kent and there was a ready market for the finished products in the City, just across London Bridge.

The wall of the Marshalsea Prison, where Charles Dickens's parents were detained as debtors, a source of great sorrow and shame to the novelist. (Wikimedia Commons, Gordon Joly)

3

Leadenhall Market: From Fruit and Veg to *Harry Potter*

The first reference to the 'Leaden Hall' occurs in a document of 1296 though by 1309, according to John Stow, it was the property of Sir Hugh Neville and his wife Alice who had erected a mansion with a lead-covered roof. A few years later it was the site of a poultry market whose traders were later joined by cheese-makers. Its site, however, was much more ancient since it occupied the site of the former Roman Basilica and forum in the very centre of the Roman Londinium. It was the largest such site north of the Alps and the market that the forum accommodated would have occupied an area the size of Trafalgar Square. In 1408, again according to John Stow:

> Robert Rikeden of Essex and Margaret his wife confirmed to Richard Whittington and other citizens of London the manor of Leaden Hall. In 1411 Richard Whittington confirmed the same manor to the mayor and commonalty of London, whereby it came to the possession of the City.

Richard Whittington thereby acquired Leadenhall, as he came to the end of the third of his four mayoralties, and passed on its ownership to the City Corporation, where it remains. In 1419 it became the site of the City's granary, a fine stone building, together with three schools and a chapel for those doing business at what had now evidently become an important centre of trade in grain. There was also a beam, similar to that in the Steelyard (see page 64) for the weighing of wool, which suggests that the market had become an important centre for trading in a variety of commodities including linen cloth and metal objects such as key rings and nails. In 1488 it was decreed that, within the City, leather could only be sold at Leadenhall. By the 1500s meat, poultry and fish were also being sold there and in 1622 it was granted a monopoly in the sale of cutlery. It had, by this time, become London's biggest market for general produce.

Entrance to Leadenhall market, 2005. (Wikimedia Commons.Yewenyi)

'Frenchman and foreigners'

In 1484 the building was severely damaged by fire but it must have been rebuilt very soon afterwards because in 1503 City merchants petitioned the Lord Mayor and Corporation to decree that all 'Frenchmen and foreigners' should be obliged to sell their wares only at the Leaden Hall and use its beam for weighing their produce. The word 'foreigners' probably meant anyone from outside the City itself. Later in the century, in 1534, as Richard Gresham tried to find premises for a *bourse* like the one he had seen in Antwerp, where merchants could trade with one another in a variety of commodities, it was suggested that Leaden Hall would be a suitable site. The alleys around Lombard Street were no longer thought to be adequate for the purpose but after some debate, in Stow's words, 'John Champneis being Mayor, it was fully concluded that the *bourse* should remain in Lombard Street, as before, and Leaden Hall no more to be spoken of concerning that matter'. Stow recorded that by his time the market was mostly devoted to wool, by far England's greatest export, and also for materials used in City pageants as well as being used as an arsenal for the storage of guns to protect the City in the event of attack. It came into its own at Christmas when, again according to Stow, a tree was 'set up in the pavement nailed full of Holly and Ivy for disport of Christmas to the people'.

Leadenhall is one of the highest points within the Square Mile and for this reason it became the site of a conduit which received water pumped up to it by a waterwheel installed in 1582 in one of the arches of London Bridge by Peter Morice, a Dutch (or possibly German) engineer. From this high point the water was distributed by gravity throughout the City. The original water-wheel was destroyed in the Great Fire of 1665 but its replacement, designed by Morice's grandson, remained in place until it was demolished along with the old London Bridge in 1822. The Great Fire of 1665 also severely damaged the market but it was once again swiftly rebuilt and was divided into three sections, all of them operating under a covered market. The first section, known as the Beef Market was devoted to the sale of beef, leather, wool and hides; the second sold veal, mutton, lamb, fish, cheese and poultry; and the third, described as the Herb Market, sold fruit and vegetables.

Diagon Alley

This market flourished until 1881 when it was demolished and rebuilt to a design by Sir Horace Jones, the City architect also responsible for Smithfield, Billingsgate and Tower Bridge. The new market was constructed of glass and wrought iron painted in green, maroon and cream in place of the former stone structure though the ornate entrance from Gracechurch Street is of Portland stone. It was extensively refurbished in 1991 and remains primarily a

Leadenhall Market, 2010. (Wikimedia Commons, Aurelien Guichard)

Leadenhall market, 2006. (Wikimedia Commons, Diliff)

food market selling meat, poultry, fruit and vegetables though it now includes florists, booksellers, wine bars, cafes and restaurants which are frequented by City workers. It is open Monday to Saturday and its distinctive architecture has earned it a place in films, becoming 'Diagon Alley' in *Harry Potter and the Philosopher's Stone* and also featuring in the film *The Imaginarium of Doctor Parnassus*. It also formed part of the 2012 Olympic Marathon course as a link for the runners between Lime Street and Whittington Avenue.

4

Sir Thomas Gresham and the Royal Exchange: London's Financial Centre

The Royal Exchange is the handsome classical building that stands at the junction of Threadneedle Street and Cornhill, opposite the Bank of England in the heart of the City. The present building, with its striking pediment and elegant columns topped by Corinthian capitals was opened by Queen Victoria in 1844 and is the third building on this site, the first having been opened by Queen Elizabeth I. It has a strong claim to have been the origin of London's position as the world's leading financial market and owes its foundation to Sir Thomas Gresham (1518–79) though the idea stemmed from Thomas's father Sir Richard.

'The meetings were unpleasant and troublesome'

Sir Richard Gresham (1494–1549) was a Merchant Adventurer, a guild of merchants who in 1407 had received a charter from King Henry IV that permitted them to export and import a range of goods, much of the trade being in cloth. Most of them were members of the Mercers Company, London's grandest livery company, which had counted Richard Whittington amongst its members and had built its great wealth on the trade in English woollen cloth or 'Mercery'.

London's Livery Companies

These companies originated in Anglo-Saxon England and became, for monarchs, a means of raising taxes from their members, regulating standards (such as the quality of bread and meat) and controlling entry to their professions by suitably qualified people. There are at present 108 livery companies from farriers and spectacle makers to information technologists and hackney carriage (taxi) drivers. Their roles are now largely social, charitable and ceremonial. In the sixteenth century an order of precedence was established with the Mercers, the grandest company, being allocated the first place. Besides Richard Whittington their members have included Geoffrey Chaucer and Sir Thomas More. The Skinners and Merchant Taylors alternate between sixth and seventh place (hence the expression 'at sixes and sevens'). Many of the livery companies have magnificent halls. These include the Mercers in Ironmonger Lane; the Goldsmiths in Foster Lane; the Founders in Cloth Fair; and the Barber-Surgeons in the Barbican. They are occasionally open to the public, for example during London's 'open house' weekends in September. The Great Twelve companies, which take precedence over all others, as determined by the Court of Aldermen in 1515 are, in order:

1. Mercers
2. Grocers
3. Drapers
4. Fishmongers
5. Goldsmiths
6. Merchant Taylors
7. Skinners
8. Haberdashers
9. Salters
10. Ironmongers
11. Vintners
12. Clothworkers

The Great Twelve companies participate by right in the annual Lord Mayor's Show, other livery companies joining the procession by invitation.

The trade in wool and cloth took Sir Richard Gresham, who himself served as Lord Mayor of London, to Antwerp, the centre of the cloth trade, whose *bourse*, or trading hall, impressed him as a fine place in which to conduct business. On his return Richard petitioned Henry VIII's chancellor, Thomas Cromwell, to support the creation of a similar facility in London, writing:

> The last year I showed your lordship a platte [plan] that was drawn out for to make a goodly burse [*bourse*] in Lombard Street for merchants to repair unto which shall be very beautiful for the City and also for the honour of our sovereign Lord the King.

Though the king gave his support, no suitable site was found and the idea lapsed when Cromwell fell from favour and was executed. The cause was taken up after Richard's death by his son, Thomas, who was himself a merchant adventurer. The need for such a building was expressed by John Stow (1525–1605) whose *Survey of London*, published in 1603, described the earlier difficulties of doing business in London's burgeoning business community without a *bourse* like Antwerp's. Stow would have witnessed the encounters he describes:

> The merchants and tradesmen, as well English as strangers, for their general making of bargains, contracts and commerce, did usually meet twice every day. But the meetings were unpleasant and troublesome by reason of walking and talking in an open street, being there constrained to endure all extremes of weather.

Gresham's Law

Thomas Gresham was more persistent than his father. Having taking over the family's Mercery business he made many visits to Antwerp and quickly discovered that his trade was suffering from the fact that English coinage had been debased by Henry VIII and his son Edward VI. They had reduced its value by adding base metals to gold and silver coins, thereby increasing the quantity of money in circulation at the expense of its quality. Continental merchants were

This grasshopper, outside a bank in Lombard Street, is the family emblem of Sir Thomas Gresham, creator of London as a financial centre. (Wikimedia Commons, Joseph Renalias)

wary of receiving payment in the debased currency and charged a premium for accepting it. Gresham coined the phrase, 'Bad money tends to drive out good', in reference to the fact that merchants with good and debased coins would always tend to offer the debased currency in payment in order to rid themselves of it. He persuaded the new queen, Elizabeth I, that allowing the currency to be adulterated was an attractive short-term measure with harmful long-term consequences since it also made it much harder to raise loans from foreign investors who feared being repaid in currency that had lost some of its value. The currency was restored and the queen appointed Thomas as Royal Agent in Antwerp, with the task of raising loans there. He was, in effect, managing the National Debt as Chancellors of the Exchequer would later do and, by offering payment in sound currency, gained better terms for repayment than had been available to the queen's predecessors. For these services he was knighted and the favour that he had gained at Elizabeth's court strengthened his hand when he revived his father's plan to give London a *bourse*.

The Royal Exchange

In 1565 the owners of thirty-six houses in Cornhill, mostly clothworkers, were informed that they had to move out to make room for a new building.

Cornhill, Lombard Street and the Mansion House, 1810. The entrance to the Royal Exchange, in the background, is surmounted by a cupola. (Ackermann)

Gresham had earned the support of Elizabeth and of 750 London merchants who raised the money to pay off the evicted householders with £3,767 6s, which one hopes was adequate compensation for the loss of their homes. Construction began in 1566, paid for by Gresham. John Stow, who probably witnessed the event, left an account of the building's opening by Queen Elizabeth I:

> In the year 1570, on 23rd January, the Queen's Majesty, attended with her Nobility, came from her house at the Strand called Somerset House and entered the City by Temple Bar, Fleet Street, Cheapside, through Threadneedle [Street], to Sir Thomas Gresham's in Bishopsgate Street, where she dined. After dinner her Majesty, returning through Cornhill, entered the Bourse [i.e. the exchange] on the south side and after she had viewed every part thereof she caused the same Bourse by a Herald and a Trumpet to be proclaimed the Royal Exchange and so to be called from thenceforth.

The queen also proclaimed that the exchange would have a licence to sell alcohol, which, over the centuries, was often used to oil the wheels of commerce in London's financial markets.

All of these street names remain in use though Temple Bar, the boundary between the City and Westminster, was removed from the Strand in the nineteenth century as an obstruction to traffic and has more recently been relocated to a position close to the north-west corner of St Paul's Cathedral. The new exchange consisted of a magnificent hall and piazza, the latter paved with Turkish stone, surrounded by arcades with statues of monarchs. Prominent amongst them was a statue of the queen herself, which was subsequently moved to the entrance to the London Guildhall Library. Nations and trades were allocated to various 'walks' of the piazza, with Norway and New England occupying spaces on the west side, Jews and Armenians on the east, and Scots and Irish to the north while grocers and ship-brokers were in the centre of the site. Small booths, measuring 5ft by 7ft, were eagerly rented by tenants who included haberdashers, goldsmiths, mercers, stationers and, from the earliest days, traders in financial services like loans and insurance. The first recorded life insurance policy was taken out on 18 June 1583 by Richard Martin on the life of William Gibbons, a London salter (supplier of salt and salted meat) at a premium of £8 per £100 for twelve months. It was supported by sixteen underwriters. It is not known whether Gibbons survived the twelve months but his salted products must have been very important to someone. The creation of a sound currency and the opening of the Royal Exchange represented significant steps in establishing London as a centre of international finance.

The Second and Third Exchange

The building was destroyed in the Great Fire but swiftly rebuilt and reopened in 1669. Sir Christopher Wren proposed to make it the centrepiece of his plan for the City. Wren's plan was never carried out since too many property owners wanted to preserve their interests against the architect's plans for broad boulevards and vistas but his plan reflected the importance that the exchange had assumed in the first century of its existence. The new exchange had an ornate entrance with a fine tower between porticos and a slightly smaller piazza than the first exchange, to make room for wider arcades to shelter traders striking bargains. It also had more enclosed booths to accommodate the rising number of would-be tenants. The vaults of the new building were let to bankers and to the East India Company as a store for its stocks of pepper, while the growing status of the building as a financial centre was reflected in the fact that Lloyd's insurance brokers eventually became tenants in addition to the traders who had occupied the original building. In the last decade of the seventeenth century dealers in stocks were banned from the exchange because of their 'loitering and gambling' and were obliged to conduct their trade from coffee houses.

Coffee Houses

London's first coffee stall was opened in 1652 by a Greek called Pasqua Rosee on St Michael's Alley, off Cornhill where its former location is marked by a blue plaque. Rosee had worked in Smyrna (now Izmir in Turkey) where he had tasted the bitter Turkish beverage and imported it to London. He advertised the new drink as excellent for digestion and a remedy for sore eyes, headache, dropsy, gout, scurvy and a multitude of other ills. Within ten years there were eighty coffee houses within the City of London alone and they quickly became fashionable gathering places where men (not women) would discuss the affairs of the day including business and politics. Coffee houses, which often charged an entrance fee for those wishing to use their facilities, also provided domestic and foreign newspapers, news-sheets, journals and bulletin boards on which were posted details of shipments arriving or lost, prices of commodities and auction notices. 'Coffee-house politicians' were of concern to Charles II, who tried to suppress them, but their rise was irresistible and some of them were the origins of institutions that became permanent features of the City. Stocks and shares were first traded in coffee houses near the Royal Exchange while Lloyd's Coffee House on Lombard Street (later occupied by Sainsbury's) gave rise to the Lloyd's insurance market.

Auctions at coffee houses were the precursors of the salerooms of dealers like Christie's and Sotheby's while habitués of the Bedford coffee house in Covent Garden passed verdict on the latest plays. In the eighteenth century, gentlemen's clubs, some of them developed from rival chocolate houses, began to take over some of the functions of the coffee houses, an example being White's in St James's Street which was started by an Italian immigrant called Francesco Bianco (Francis White). So Starbucks and Caffe Nero are nothing new.

Perhaps it was the 'loitering and gambling' of dealers in stocks which caused Dr Samuel Johnson, in his *Dictionary* to define a stockjobber as, 'A low wretch who gets money by buying and selling shares in the funds'. Nevertheless, the importance of the Royal Exchange and its international character were reflected in an article in an early edition of *The Spectator*, written by one of the magazine's founders, Joseph Addison, in May 1711:

There is no place in the town which I so much love to frequent as the Royal Exchange. It gives me a secret satisfaction and in some measure gratifies my vanity as I am an Englishman to see so rich an Assembly of Countrymen and Foreigners, consulting together upon the private business of Mankind and making this Metropolis a kind of Emporium for the whole earth. Sometimes I am jostled by a body of Armenians, sometimes I am lost in a crowd of Jews or Dutchmen, sometimes Danes, Swedes or Frenchmen.

'Selfishness and avarice'

A revised edition of Stow's *Survey of London*, published in the eighteenth century, explained how the new exchange worked: 'for the most easy expediting of their work, the merchants dealing in the same Commodities have by custom fixed on these different Parts of the Exchange to meet one another, called Walks'. So there was a Norway Walk, Virginia Walk, Jamaica Walk, Spanish Walk and Jews' Walk. In time, some of the activities of the exchange, such as insurance and stockbroking, became so great that they migrated to their own specialist venues but in the eighteenth century the exchange and its surrounding streets were the commercial heart of the City. The favourable impression made upon Addison was not universally shared. In 1826 Prince Hermann Puckler-Muskau, an impecunious Saxon nobleman, inveterate traveller, gardener and socialite, visited London in search of a wealthy wife to support his ambitions and, although he was impressed by the 'stately architecture' of the exchange, thought little of its occupants:

The Royal Exchange. (Wikimedia Commons, Aurelian Guichard)

> The men, however, who animate the picture, soon draw one back into the region of commonplace, for selfishness and avarice gleam but too clearly from every eye. In this point of view the place I am describing, and indeed the whole City, have a repulsive, sinister aspect, which almost remind one of the restless and comfortless throng of the spirits of the damned.

Perhaps he was disillusioned by his failure to find a suitable wife, though he was later comforted by a teenage slave girl whom he purchased in the market in Cairo and named Mahbuba, the Beloved.

The building survived until another fire destroyed it in January 1838. The present building, designed by Sir William Tite, was opened in 1844 by Queen Victoria whose own statue, and one of Sir Thomas Gresham himself, were added to those of other monarchs that had survived the second fire. A further reminder of the founder is the exchange's weathervane, which is in the form of a grasshopper, taken from the Gresham family coat of arms. For the first time a Metal Exchange moved into the new building, a further sign of London's increasing ascendancy as the world's leading trading centre. A cache of Roman coins discovered when the foundations were being built is now in the Museum of London. There is one conspicuous survival from the original exchange: the central 'Turkish' courtyard.

Final Days

The Royal Exchange ceased to function as a market in 1939, its activities having been taken over by specialist operations like the Stock Exchange, Lloyd's and the Baltic Exchange. For many years after the Second World War it served as an office for the Guardian Royal Exchange Insurance Company and was regarded by many as an under-used asset on one of the most valuable sites in the world. From 1982 to 1991 it was the home of the London International Financial Futures Exchange (LIFFE) whose traders in their loud, striped jackets with their even louder 'open outcry' methods of doing business made the trading floor one of the noisiest places in the City. When LIFFE moved to new premises the Royal Exchange was redeveloped as a luxurious retail centre where you are more likely to find Gucci handbags, Tiffany jewellery and Hermes fragrances than the merchandise of those earliest tenants who followed the trades of haberdasher and stationer. In front of the exchange is one of many statues of the Duke of Wellington on horseback but this one is unique in one embarrassing respect: the sculptor forgot to give him any spurs!

WHEN CAN I VISIT?

The Exchange Retail Centre is open daily from 10 a.m. to 6 p.m., cafes and restaurants opening from 8 a.m. to 11 p.m. with clothing shops, jewellers, cafes, wine bars and restaurants open to anyone who wants to buy or gaze. It has its own website giving details of all its retailers at www.theroyalexchange.com.

Gresham College

The Royal Exchange was not Sir Thomas's only enduring legacy to the City. He also endowed Gresham College, with seven professors to deliver free public lectures from a site that was on the present site of Tower 42 (formerly the NatWest Tower) off Bishopsgate. Christopher Wren was one of its early professors. The Royal Society arose from a discussion at Gresham College in 1660 and after several moves Gresham College is now based in Barnard's Inn, Holborn, where free lectures continue to be given by distinguished public figures. Chancery Lane Station is close by. The website, which gives details of the lectures, is to be found at www.gresham.ac.uk.

5

'Our Word Our Bond': The Baltic Exchange and the World's Shipping

It is a great misfortune that London's Baltic Exchange is remembered less for its pre-eminent role in world shipping markets than for a disaster inflicted upon it on 10 April 1992, the day after the general election of that year. As voters heard of the unexpected re-election of the Conservative government of John Major, a bomb, planted by the Provisional IRA, detonated at 9.20 p.m. outside the Baltic Exchange's Grade II listed building at No. 30 St Mary Axe. It killed three people and destroyed the fine façade of the exchange and much of its Exchange Hall. There followed a long and often contentious argument between the exchange, architectural conservationists, the City Corporation, English Heritage and, eventually, the government about the future of the ruined building. At first, English Heritage insisted that the building, and particularly its elegant façade on St Mary Axe, should be restored to its original condition and appearance but surveys indicated that the destruction wrought by the explosion made this either impossible or prohibitively expensive. The remains of the building were carefully dismantled and sold in 2003 to a company trading in architectural salvage, which stored them in Cheshire before selling them on to a specialist dealer who moved them to a location near Canterbury in Kent. They included the entire façade of Portland stone; sixteen marble columns, each weighing 4 tons; and plaster mouldings from the exchange's trading hall depicting sea monsters, mermaids and similar sea creatures. In 2006 Eerik-Niiles Kross, an Estonian diplomat, businessman and Estonian patriot with a record of resistance to the Soviet occupiers of his country, found the salvaged materials on the web by chance and purchased them for about £800,000. They were taken to a highly appropriate home at Tallinn, the capital of the Baltic Republic of Estonia, where Kross wishes to reconstruct them as a centrepiece of the city's commercial sector though this plan has attracted some opposition from the National Heritage Board of Estonia.

The Gherkin, more prosaically known as No. 30 St Mary Axe, which now occupies the former site of the Baltic Exchange. (Wikimedia Commons, Mario Roberto Duran Ortiz)

The Gherkin

The site of the ruined exchange was sold to the property company Trafalgar House, which wrestled long with the problems that accompany any new building in the City of London. The most formidable of these is that they must not obstruct views of St Paul's Cathedral from a number of locations around the City and must not interfere with flight paths to Heathrow. Finally, after a series of failed planning applications, the company was granted permission by John Prescott in August 2000 for a building that, after further misadventures in the planning process, was to become one of the City's most iconic structures. Designed by the architect Norman Foster and the engineers Arup it opened it 2004 having become known, from an early stage of its construction, as The Gherkin because of its distinctive shape. It is also known as The Swiss Re Building after its principal occupant, a Swiss reinsurance company though its postal address is the more mundane No. 30, St Mary Axe. Its topmost panoramic dome is known as The Lens and recalls the glass dome that covered the Exchange Hall of the Baltic Exchange before its destruction. It is appropriate that the former home of one of London's most important markets should be occupied by one of the City's most distinctive buildings following the destruction caused in April 1992. The Baltic Exchange's motto remains 'Our Word Our Bond', similar to that of the Stock Exchange's *Dictum Meum Pactum*, 'My Word is My Bond'.

The Virginia and Baltick Coffee House

In 1994 the Baltic Exchange celebrated its 250th anniversary, its origins traditionally lying in an announcement which appeared in *The Daily Post* on 25 May 1744 of a decision by the owners of The Maryland Coffee House to change its name to reflect the fact that it had become the principal gathering place of merchants and shipowners who were trading with the Baltic ports. The announcement was short and to the point:

> This is to give notice that the house, late the Maryland Coffee House in Threadneedle Street, near the Royal Exchange, is now opened by the name of the Virginia and Baltic Coffee House where all foreign and domestic news are taken in and all letters or parcels directed to merchants or captains of the Virginia or Baltic trade will be delivered according as directed.

The notice was immediately followed by the claim that the Coffee House also offered 'Punch, made in any Quality, in the greatest Perfection'.

The Virginia and Baltick Coffee House did not, at this stage, enjoy the exclusive attention of shipping merchants as can be seen in an advertisement for Garraway's Coffee House in 1751:

> For Sale by the Candle at Garraway's Coffee House in Exchange Alley, Cornhill

In about eight days, the following Goods, viz.

100 tons fine, unchipped, Honduras Longwood

32 tons ditto chipped

12 Casks Carolina Indigo

And other goods

Catalogues of which will be timely dispersed by Mark Hudson, Sworn Broker in

Lawrence Pountney Lane, Cannon Street.

'Sale by the Candle' meant that the auction went on as long as a candle burned. Garraway's Coffee House later became a home for stockbrokers when they were banned from the Royal Exchange for misbehaviour. Garraway's survived until the nineteenth century and the name endures as that of a coffee merchant.

In reality the origins of the exchange may be traced back much further, into the mediaeval period. In 1381, in a year more often associated with the Peasants' Revolt, King Richard II proclaimed that English merchants must import and export produce only in vessels of 'the king's allegiance' – in other words in ships owned by English subjects. This early manifestation of protectionist restraints on trade was primarily designed to ensure that England had a flourishing fleet of merchant vessels that could, if necessary, be converted to vessels of war in conflict with France, the Hundred Years' War then being almost halfway through its course. In 1488 Henry VII's Navigation Act reinforced these requirements and although they were relaxed by his granddaughter, Elizabeth I, they were renewed and strengthened by Oliver Cromwell's 'Maritime Charter of England' in 1651. The charter, which was renewed by Charles II, remained in force, though often circumvented, until 1839 when free trade had replaced protectionism as Britain's economic credo. The measures were nevertheless instrumental in establishing a large and powerful British merchant fleet that underpinned the market for chartering vessels for which the Baltic Exchange was to become renowned.

Baltic Trade

In the meantime other steps had been taken to promote English trade with the Baltic. Henry IV, who had deposed Richard II in 1399 (and probably had him murdered) granted royal letters of privilege to a company of Baltic Adventurers, a short-lived enterprise whose existence served mainly to reflect the importance of England's trade with the area, mostly in timber, hemp, tar and tallow for the construction of ships and ropes. In 1555 Queen Mary, in one of her rare constructive acts, granted a charter to the Muscovy Company, the first English joint-stock company (i.e. with shareholders) engaged in trade. The company prospered and was very active in Baltic trade in the reign of Elizabeth I, survived until the Russian Revolution of 1917 and now operates as a charity. By 1685 over a hundred English merchants were sufficiently active in the Baltic to be trading in more than £500 worth of goods each year, a sum equivalent to about £700,000 in the twenty-first century. The best known of these, Gilbert Heathcote, described as 'The richest commoner in England' became Lord Mayor of London in 1711. In the latter part of the eighteenth century the trade was further promoted as a result of a series of good harvests, especially in East Anglia from which much of the trade was conducted. The government subsidised exports of grain by payments of 5s per quarter (28 pounds or 12.7 kilos) of grain, leading to further demands for shipping in London's coffee houses.

So by 1744, the date of the announcement in *The Daily Post*, Britain had both a flourishing merchant fleet, helped in part by the Navigation Acts, and strong links with the Baltic. In the years that lay ahead, trade with other parts of the world such as the American colonies, the Empire and Western Europe far surpassed that with the Baltic ports but the name stuck and moved with the merchants as they proceeded to occupy a variety of premises in the City. There was at this time no formal organisation or membership, simply a fraternity of merchants, British and foreign, who regularly gathered to drink coffee and do business. In 1810 the number of transactions had reached a level too great for the Virginia and Baltick Coffee House to accommodate so the merchants moved to the larger Antwerp Tavern, also in Threadneedle Street, which obligingly changed its name to The Baltic Coffee House to reflect the fact that it had supplanted the nearby Virginia and Baltic Coffee House as the principal centre for Baltic trade. It attracted shipowners, ship brokers and merchants who sought means of conveying cargoes of all kinds though timber, hemp, tar and tallow continued to predominate in trade between the Baltic ports and those of the East coast of England, especially East Anglia. The business received a further boost with the repeal of the Corn Laws by Sir Robert Peel's government in 1846. The laws had used tariffs to protect Britain's farmers against cheaper grain from the United States and Australia and their repeal, though controversial at the time, opened Britain's markets to free trade. This reduced the price of food and led to a huge increase in shipping, not only from London, but also from other major ports such as Liverpool, which has its own Baltic Square, as does Gateshead on the Tyne.

'Wild gambling'

By this time scandal had begun to envelop the exchange, much of it associated with a man called Richard Thornton. Born in 1775 he died at the age of

90 leaving a fortune variously estimated as between £2 million and £4 million, the equivalent of £140 million to £280 million at present values. This was attributed to his activities as 'an unscrupulous cornerer of [the market in] tallow', a product that was essential for the manufacture of candles and as a lubricant for early steam engines before oil became available. It was in an attempt to combat the 'wild gambling' of traders like Thornton that, in 1823, a group of coffee house regulars formed a committee which drafted a set of rules governing admission to what was now becoming a formal organisation. A maximum of 300 subscribers paid a fee of four guineas (£4.20) to gain admission to a 'subscription room' where transactions were carried out. Non-subscribers were still admitted to dining and coffee rooms, as with the coffee houses, but by restricting entry to the Subscription Room, which was in effect the trading floor, they were creating a new and more formal market.

They now began to look for their own premises from which to trade and in 1857 they formed a company to purchase South Sea House, also in Threadneedle Street. Originally the home of the South Sea Company, which had been responsible for the speculative frenzy that produced the South Sea Bubble of 1720, it later became the premises of the Royal British Bank, which suffered a similar fate in 1856, thus leaving the building available for the Baltic merchants. They adopted the name 'The Baltic Company' even though by 1857 most of the trade was with the burgeoning British Empire in warmer seas than the chilly Baltic. History and sentiment prevailed over hard commercial logic.

Thornton wasn't the only notable character associated with the Baltic Exchange in the mid-nineteenth century. John Osborne, the tyrannical, ruthless and snobbish father of the disreputable George in Thackeray's *Vanity Fair*, frequented the Baltic Exchange and at about the same time, in 1845, Paul Julius Reuter arrived in London and set up his news agency, using the new telegraphs, which made it easier to transmit news and prices and thereby made it harder for people like Thornton to corner markets. At this time the exchange benefited from Britain's ascendancy in industrial output and foreign trade, its economy fuelled by imports of raw materials from the Empire and the export of manufactured goods. Britain accounted for one third of total global manufactures and a proportionate amount of shipping, all of it arranged through the Baltic Exchange.

Paul Julius Reuter (1816–99)

Reuter was born in Germany as Israel Josaphat. He came to England in 1845, was baptised Paul Julius Reuter and made ingenious use of carrier pigeons and the new telegraphs to gather and transmit news, especially financial news, amongst the world's major centres, with offices in London, Paris and Berlin. After some resistance British newspapers, led by the *Morning Post*, began to purchase his services and he was the first to report the assassination of Abraham Lincoln in 1865. In the same year he floated Reuters as a public company, many of the shares being bought by newspaper groups. In 2008 the business was bought by the Thomson Corporation and the founder's last descendant, Baroness Marguerite de Reuter, died in 2009, aged 96.

South Sea House and a Growing Membership

From the earliest days at South Sea House foreign merchants and shipowners were admitted to a growing membership, with Greeks and Germans particularly prominent. This enterprise caused some embarrassment during the First World War when the membership of German firms and individuals was suspended, a measure that, though inevitable in the circumstances, caused some misgivings amongst their British colleagues, with whom they had worked harmoniously for years. This did not prevent a 'howl of indignation' being heard from the Exchange Hall when news arrived of the sinking of the *Lusitania* by a German U-boat in May 1915, with the loss of almost 1,200 lives, an act which helped to draw the United States into the First World War. The present membership of the exchange amounts to about 600 companies (about two thirds based in the United Kingdom) and 3,000 individuals. The membership includes a shipbroking business called Harris and Dixon, which joined the gatherings at the coffee house in 1797, sixty years before South Sea House became the exchange's home. The business continues to survive as the world's oldest shipbrokers, now trading from premises in Southwark and specialising in cruise ships. Harris and Dixon's contracts customarily opened with the words, 'It is this day mutually agreed ...' a form of words soon adopted by other traders and still in use.

In the meantime more pressing anxieties had arisen nearer to home. One of these was caused by the launching of Isambard Kingdom Brunel's *Great Eastern* in January 1858. Brunel already had a formidable reputation as the designer of the *Great Britain* and other vessels whose size, speed and capacity exceeded any previously seen but the *Great Eastern* was in another league. At almost 700ft long and weighing over 18,000 tons it was more than forty years before any other vessel exceeded it in size and the problems and anxieties associated with its construction and launch hastened Brunel's early death the following year. Its launch from Millwall was witnessed by 3,000 spectators and was marked by a series of accidents to participants, while its maiden voyage was marred by an explosion that caused the deaths of five crewmembers. It was designed to carry 4,000 passengers to Australia without refuelling and its size was such that there were doubts about whether it could be accommodated in many of the world's ports or, indeed, in the Suez Canal when that was being constructed. The Baltic shipbrokers doubted whether they would be able to find much use for it but were reassured when, after a number of failed ventures, it ended its days as a cable-laying vessel, laying the first telegraphic cable from Europe to the United States and subsequently reaching as far as Bombay (Mumbai). The ship was scrapped at a workshop on the Wirral peninsula in Merseyside in 1890 and fragments of it are still occasionally found on the shores of the Mersey. Its topmast survives as a flagpole at Liverpool's Anfield football ground.

In 1900 the Baltic Exchange bought the London Shipping Exchange, a rival organisation that had briefly flourished in the 1890s and the new, larger body sought a new permanent home. The directors found a site in Jeffrey's Square, now Saint Mary Axe, and purchased it for £87,693.

The Church of St Mary Axe

This church was built in about 1197 and suppressed in 1560, its site later being occupied by a warehouse. It owes its name to a legend that the daughter of an unnamed English king travelled along the Rhine with 11,000 handmaidens. It was their misfortune to encounter Attila the Hun, a man not noted for his tender disposition, who beheaded them with three axes, one of which was supposedly to be found in the church named after the events.

The lease on South Sea House expired in 1900 and the new company, the Baltic Mercantile and Shipping Exchange Ltd, its shares owned by its members, occupied a temporary home in the Great Eastern Hotel, adjacent to Liverpool Street Station, while the new premises at No. 30, St Mary Axe, were being built by the London architects T.H. Smith and W. Wimble. On 21 April 1903 the new exchange opened, to reveal one of the City's finest buildings. Its façade on St Mary Axe was in red granite while its Exchange Hall, where merchants, shipowners and ship brokers transacted business for over half of the world's shipping and a similar proportion of the world's sales of vessels, was one of the largest rooms in the City. It was lavishly decorated in marble, mahogany and stained glass. The exchange is governed by a board of twelve to fifteen directors, mostly elected by holders of shares in the company.

The Baltic Exchange in the Twenty-First Century

Besides facilitating trade between merchants and shipowners, the Baltic Exchange also publishes a number of maritime shipping indices of which the most important is the daily Baltic Dry Index, which it describes as, 'an assessment of the price of moving the major raw materials by sea'. It operates like the Financial Times Stock Exchange (FTSE) Index by recording prices paid for the transport of cargoes in a multitude of transactions and calculating movements in the prices from hour to hour and day to day. About half of the cargoes brokered at the exchange, measured by weight, are energy generating: oil, coal and liquefied gas, followed by foodstuffs, fertilisers and construction materials. Container traffic is only about 10 per cent by weight but much more by value. The Index enables those who wish to transport bulk commodities to judge the likely cost of moving them across the world's oceans and, by tracking movements in the Index, to judge whether to conclude a deal immediately or, if trends seem favourable, to wait for a few days in the hope that shipping rates will fall. Such decisions can be critical. At times of crisis, as when the Suez Canal closed in 1956, shipping rates can soar in a matter of days or hours while a fall in world trade and economic activity can release a large volume of empty vessels bidding for cargoes at falling prices. On 20 May 2008, at the height of the economic boom, the Baltic Dry Index reached a record level of 11,793. By 5 December the same year, following the financial crisis signalled by the collapse of Lehman brothers on 15 September, it had fallen by 95 per cent to 663. It can be accessed on the web by entering 'Baltic Dry Index' into a search engine and is as good a way as any of monitoring the world's economic health. Since 1929 the chartering of aircraft has been added to the activities of the exchange.

A New Home

In 1995 the exchange moved to new premises at No. 38, St Mary Axe, a few doors from the building destroyed by the Provisional IRA in 1992 and in the shadow of the Gherkin which occupies the site of its former home. It continues to play a dominant role in world shipping and its trading floor, unlike many in the City which have given way to computerised trading, continues to host face to face transactions. It is possible to organise visits to the exchange by contacting 0207 283 9300 or e-mailing: enquiries@balticexchange.com.

6

Famous for Fish and Foul Language: Billingsgate

Billingsgate, close to the site of the Monument to the Great Fire of 1665, was not always London's premier fish market. Although records of fish being landed on Billingsgate's quays date from the early eleventh century it struggled to compete as a landing place for fish with Queenhithe which still exists as a ward of the City, just upstream beyond London Bridge. The word *hithe* is Anglo-Saxon and means a small port or haven. Queenhithe acquired its name when Matilda, the daughter of Henry I (1100–1135) whom Henry expected to succeed him as monarch, was granted duties on produce landed there. The desire to protect this source of royal revenue caused successive monarchs to penalise rival wharfs, including Billingsgate. The completion of the mediaeval London Bridge in 1209 made it more difficult for small craft to pass through the bridge to Queenhithe because of the rapid rush of water through the many narrow arches and even more difficult for larger vessels. Billingsgate, downstream from the bridge, therefore became so much more attractive that in 1227 Henry III ordered the Constable of the City 'to detain all fish offered to be sold in any place of this City but at the Queenhithe'. This order, widely evaded, was later modified to allow fish to be landed at Billingsgate if there was more than one vessel waiting to be unloaded at Queenhithe. Besides fish, much else was landed at Billingsgate. The *Liber Albus* (see page 12), compiled by John Carpenter in 1419, sets out regulations concerning the sale of malt at Billingsgate as well as recording the costs of docking there and landing cargoes:

> Two [old] pence for docking a large vessel
> One penny for docking a small vessel
> One farthing per thousand herrings 'entering or exported' [a farthing being a quarter of an old penny]
> Twelve pence per ton of honey [clearly Billingsgate wasn't only for fish; details of charges were also given for iron, onions, garlic, flax and other commodities]

Billingsgate Market, 1808, conducted on the quayside by stallholders. (Thomas Rowlandson)

A Warning to Others

Carpenter also recorded other regulations concerning the market. Thus 'No-one shall buy fish in any vessel afloat until the ropes are brought on shore', presumably because vessels didn't pay their docking dues until they were roped to the quayside and the authorities didn't want them to escape without payment. More curiously, 'No man shall sell or buy fresh fish for resale before sunrise or salt fish before the hour of Prime' ('Prime' being a time of prayer marked by the tolling of a bell of St Paul's Cathedral at about 6 a.m.). There were also rules governing the size of the mesh of nets which were designed to ensure that only fully grown fish would be caught, enabling smaller fish to escape, a conservation measure similar to those prescribed in the twenty-first century by the European Union. Those who transgressed, like Alan atte Were, were punished. His nets:

> Ought to have been two inches in width at least while small fish of the size and dimensions of one inch could not pass through them.

His nets were publicly burnt as a warning to others.

'A large Watergate, Port or Harbour'

In his *Survey of London* John Stow, in his account of London's gates, recorded that Queenhithe had been, 'the very chief and principal watergate of this city, being a common strand or landing place, yet equal with and of old times far exceeding Belins Gate' (i.e. Billingsgate). Stow surmised that the name arose from a former (probably Saxon) owner of the quay called Beling or Biling, dismissing the claim by the highly imaginative twelfth-century historian Geoffrey of Monmouth that the name predated the Christian era. Stow also recorded that the Oystergate, a small harbour on the present site of Oystergate Walk, just upstream from London Bridge, was 'the chiefest market for them [oysters] and for other shell fishes' and that by his time (he was writing about 1600) Billingsgate 'is now most frequented, the Queen's Hithe being almost forsaken'. At this time Billingsgate was used for much more than fish. In Stow's words it was:

A large Watergate, Port or Harbour for ships and boats commonly arriving there with fish, both fresh and salt, shell fish, salet [shrimps], oranges, onions and other fruits and roots, wheat, rye and grain of divers sorts for service of the City and then parts of this Realm adjoining.

The position of Billingsgate was further strengthened in the fourteenth century when the Fishmongers Company (fourth of the Great Twelve, see page 29 above) secured a monopoly of the sale of fish in the City and realised that this would be easier to exercise if the landing and marketing of fish could be centralised in one place, Billingsgate being chosen for the purpose. This did not prevent some traders from attempting to corner the market in some types of fish by buying up scarce cargoes direct from ships and thereby keeping them from Billingsgate so, after a campaign by the Fishmongers Company, an Act of Parliament declared in 1698 that:

Billingsgate, having time out of mind been a free market for all manner of floating [i.e. fresh] and salt fish, after the tenth day of May 1699 Billingsgate Market within the said City of London shall be every day in the week except the Sabbath a free and open market for all sorts of fish whatsoever.

Foul Language

From this time Billingsgate's position as London's wholesale fish market was virtually unchallenged and it flourished, though it was still an essentially free enterprise, unregulated and housed in ramshackle, makeshift sheds on the site of what later became Lower Thames Street, in the shadow of the

Monument to the Great Fire. In 1846 the City Corporation stepped in and put Billingsgate, like Smithfield, under the control of the Corporation's Markets Committee which set up a system of rents for stalls and tolls for landing fish, supervised by a Billingsgate Market Superintendent supported by a special Market Police Force. The area became crowded, noisy and rather disreputable with the crowds attracting pickpockets and the market porters acquiring a reputation for foul language as they jostled and elbowed their way amongst the narrow streets and close-packed stalls. George Orwell worked at Billingsgate in the 1930s as did the infamous Kray twins, Ronnie and Reggie, in the 1950s. Billy Walker, the heavyweight boxer whose fights attracted a substantial following in the 1960s, was also a Billingsgate porter for several years. A first attempt in the 1850s to equip the market with a suitable permanent structure by the City's architect J.B. Bunning, who had earlier built London's Coal Exchange, was not satisfactory and in 1877 a new building opened, designed by Sir Horace Jones.

Sir Horace Jones (1819–87)

Jones was responsible for designing many of the City's most famous landmarks in his capacity as architect to the City Corporation, a position to which he was appointed in 1864. Born in Bucklersbury, in the heart of the City, one of his early commissions was Caversham Park, near Reading, a stately home that he designed in 1850 and which is now the home of the BBC's monitoring service. Following his appointment as City architect his more prominent additions to the City included Billingsgate Fish Market, Smithfield Meat Market, Leadenhall and, most famously, Tower Bridge in which he was assisted by John Wolfe Barry, son of the architect of the Palace of Westminster Sir Charles Barry; and by Henry Brunel, son of the engineer Isambard Kingdom Brunel. He died seven years before the bridge was completed and the construction work was overseen by Barry and Brunel but the design was that of Horace Jones and the work for which he is best remembered.

The New Billingsgate

The new market which opened in 1877 was to a design which Jones himself described as 'Italian in character' though others have detected more of the French Renaissance School of Architecture with its fine arcades, mansard roof and golden dolphins serving as weathervanes at each end of the building. Horace Jones had also included in the design facilities for boiling shellfish which eliminated the need for cauldrons of boiling water in the open air, an obstacle and hazard to market workers and passers-by. However, the fine new building did not overcome the deficiencies of the site itself, hemmed in as it was by the Custom House and Lower Thames Street, the latter busy thoroughfare making it difficult for road vehicles to be loaded and unloaded. As early as 1883 it was claimed that, 'the deficiencies of Billingsgate and its surrounds are a great scandal to London' and the market's reputation for short tempers and bad language persisted.

It is from this time, the later nineteenth century, that we have clearer records of the produce sold at Billlingsgate and its sources. Most of the fish was brought up river from East Anglian fishing grounds, the biggest suppliers being the fishermen of Barking in Essex and the Medway towns such as Rochester and, further afield, Faversham. Colchester supplied oysters and Leigh-on-Sea brought shrimps. Well into the nineteenth century eels were still being brought by road in barrels of water from the East Anglian fenlands, the water being changed at overnight stops to ensure that the eels arrived fresh in the capital. From the 1840s fish started to arrive by rail from places as distant as Liverpool, Hull and Hartlepool, with King's Cross being the main point of arrival before transport on to Billingsgate by horse-drawn carts. By 1900 rail had overtaken boats as the principal form of transport to the market though from the 1970s rail transport had itself given way to refrigerated lorries. By the early twentieth century weekly deliveries approached 4,000 tons.

Once the fish arrived at Billingsgate they fell into the hands of the market staff, with fine distinctions in status and function matching those of their Smithfield equivalents, many of the jobs being handed down within families from one generation to the next. The aristocrats were the Fellowship Porters who could perform most tasks for most types of fish and who had a special claim on the movement of oysters. The next in line, Ticket Porters, were mostly concerned with dried and smoked fish, especially bloaters (smoked herrings); and finally the third category (variously known as 'foreigners', 'bobbers' or 'roughs') operated under the instruction of the more privileged porters or cleared up, hoping to gain elevation to a higher category when vacancies and contacts permitted. The main tasks were 'shoring in' and 'barrowing'. 'Shoring in' involved moving fish from the ships on the quay, or later from the waiting carts and lorries, to the stalls of the fish wholesalers who were known as 'fish factors' or 'salesmen'. Bargains would be struck between the 'fish factors' and their customers, these being retail fishmongers or catering outlets, including the fish and chip shops which appeared in the nineteenth century. Once an agreement had been made the fish would be 'barrowed' to the customer's waiting cart or later van.

Fish and Chips

Fish and chips became popular as a cheap and nutritious food in England in the mid-nineteenth century when fresh fish became widely available as the rapidly expanding rail network linked inland communities to fishing ports. Henry Mayhew (1812–87) who long campaigned for improvements in the living conditions of the poor, estimated that working-class diets had improved as the result of the wider availability of fresh fish. Fried fish was introduced to England by Jewish immigrants who had been invited back to England by Oliver Cromwell long after they were expelled by Edward I (who owed them money) in 1290. Chips probably originated in Belgium, the first reference to them in England occurring in Charles Dickens' *A Tale of Two Cities* where he refers to 'husky chips of potatoes fried with some reluctant drops of oil'. The first fish and chip shop was opened by a Jewish fishmonger, Joseph Malin, in Whitechapel in 1860. The dish's popularity grew in the Second World War when fish and chips was one of the few common dishes that was not rationed. It remains one of our most popular foods, with 8,600 fish and chip shops in Great Britain, though the practice of wrapping it in old newspapers was a casualty of health and safety fears of the 1970s.

Old Billingsgate Market, 2006. (Wikimedia Commons, Keith Jones)

Bobbin Money, Bobbin Hats and Bummarees

The porters were licensed by the City Corporation and their wages were paid by the wholesalers who employed them but they would also be paid 'bobbin money' by the customers to whom they transported the fish. This was paid at the rate of a 'bob' (one shilling or five pence) per stone of fish carried (14 pounds or 6.3 kilos). Because of the crowded and constricted nature of the market 'barrowing' rarely involved barrows. Instead the porters carried the fish in wooden boxes on their heads, surmounted by 'bobbin hats', a further reference to the traditional payment of a bob. The hats, also known as helmets, were very sturdy, constructed of wood, leather and tar with turned-up brims which, with the waterproofing tar, protected the wearer from water, frequently ice-cold, dripping from the boxes onto their heads and necks. These hats remained in use until the early 1960s and were, according to legend, based on the helmets worn at Agincourt by Henry V's archers.

Besides the official wholesalers there were, until the late nineteenth century, unofficial entrepreneurs known as 'bummarees', who should not be confused with their Smithfield namesakes. They would buy fish cheaply from boats that were prevented from reaching Billingsgate by unfavourable winds or tides, carry them overland by road or later rail, and sell them directly to retail outlets or to costermongers ('barrow boys') for onward sale to the public. Their activities were never recognised by the Billingsgate authorities and they were put out of business by more efficient means of transport, the term occasionally being used now to mean a middleman.

A New Home

By the 1970s the constraints of the Billingsgate site had been made worse by the widening of Lower Thames Street and on 16 January 1982 it closed. It reopened on its new site in the former West India Docks, in the shadow of Canary Wharf, when the bell brought from Old Billingsgate sounded at 4 a.m. on the following Monday, 19 January. The market, covering 13 acres, now used by about forty wholesalers, trades from Tuesday to Saturday from 4 a.m. to 9.30 a.m. and besides fish it deals in cooking oils, potatoes and other produce associated with the fish trade. The overwhelming impression made on the visitor is of the colour white: the white coats of the merchants and porters; the white tiling of the building and of the refrigerated storage and display units; and the predominantly white fish. The market now handles about 1,500 tons of fish each week, less than half the quantity handled at its peak. This is because much of its trade is now in samples, with bulk deliveries being made directly from suppliers' to customers' premises. At one time the City Corporation licensed 240 porters but the number fell to little more than

a hundred and in 2012 moves have been made to buy out the remaining porters and their ranks and customs.

Billingsgate Market, 2010. (Wikimedia Commons, Jorge Royan)

WHEN CAN I VISIT?

The market is open to any member of the public who is prepared to rise early
and drive to Trafalgar Way, London E14 5ST and escorted tours can be made
by arrangement with the management by calling 0207 987 1118 or emailing:
billingsgatemarket@cityoflondon.gov.uk.

Old Billingsgate

A campaign to preserve Old Billingsgate Market was pushing at an open door
since there was never a serious likelihood that the Grade II listed building
would be demolished. A conversion to other uses was delayed by the discovery that so much ice had been used in the basement that it had created a
permafrost effect that had first to be remedied. The building was eventually
refurbished by the architect Richard Rogers in 1988 and is now run as an
events venue with the former trading hall, where fish was traded for a century,
particularly popular for fashion shows as well as banquets, presentation cer-
emonies and conferences. Its address is No. 16, Lower Thames Street, EC3R
6DX; tel. 0207 283 2800.

7

'My Word is My Bond': the Stock Exchange and the Financial Markets

---

The London Stock Exchange is by no means the oldest of London's markets. Indeed compared with Leadenhall, Smithfield, Billingsgate and many others it is positively juvenile. But it is the largest, often the most controversial and certainly the one that has undergone the most rapid and spectacular change in the last thirty years. For a time in the early 1980s its antiquated practices meant that it was in danger of being sidelined by other markets like New York and Tokyo but the changes wrought by the Big Bang of 1986 have restored it to a central position in the global market for the trading of securities and given it a dominant position in Europe. Because of its complexity the Stock Exchange will be described in four separate sections: the early market which was conducted mostly in coffee houses and in the streets around the Royal Exchange and was subject to the loosest of regulation; the New Exchange of the nineteenth and the early twentieth century which traded from its own premises, had its own code of conduct and had many of the characteristics of a gentlemen's club; the Stock Exchange during wartime; and the modern stock market which, having emerged from the Second World War in a state of shabby complacency, was revived by the Big Bang of 1986. Each of these had its own character that merits separate analysis. It is followed by a separate section on the London International Financial Futures and Options Exchange, which, though it shares many characteristics with the Stock Exchange, has always, had its own separate identity.

8

The Coffee House Exchange

Joint Stock Companies

The first joint stock companies, owned by shareholders who could trade the shares, were created in the Tudor period. The Company of Merchant Adventurers to New Lands received its royal charter in 1553 with 250 shareholders and in 1555 was soon followed by the Muscovy Company, with a monopoly of trade to Russia. The much larger East India Company, which would effectively rule India for a time, was chartered by Elizabeth I in 1600. The companies did not enjoy limited liability, with its protection for shareholders, until an Act of 1856 but they did have the ability to raise money from a multitude of investors and could thereby create a greater financial base than could be achieved by individuals or partnerships. By the 1690s there were about 150 joint stock companies in England, enough to create a lively market in their shares. The early trading took place at coffee houses like Garraway's, which had opened in 1669 in Exchange Alley (later Change Alley), close to the present site of the Royal Exchange. Besides providing coffee Thomas Garraway also plied his customers with cherry wine, sherry, pale ale and punch. Garraway's was primarily an auction house associated with the Hudson's Bay Company, its main activities being the auctioning of sugar, coffee, textiles, rice and ships though Thomas's particular speciality was tea which he advertised as being 'for the cure of all disorders'. At this point the auctioning, buying and selling of shares in joint stock companies was a small part of the transactions conducted at Garraway's but the business flourished and is featured in many of the works of Charles Dickens including *Pickwick Papers, Martin Chuzzlewit* and *Little Dorrit*. Garraway's closed in 1872 to make way for Martin's Bank. Its former site is marked by an engraving in Change Alley, between Cornhill and Lombard Street.

Garraway's Coffee House was a general meeting place at which to discuss City affairs. Thus on 25 August 1715, a meeting was called to discuss the appalling state of the Stocks Market, a market established in about 1282 close to the City stocks, where criminals were held, hence the name. It was a market for fruit and vegetables, which was destroyed in the Great Fire of 1665, rebuilt with a fine statue of Charles II and described by John Strype in the eighteenth century as 'surpassing all other markets in London'.

John Strype (1643–1737)

Strype was born in Houndsditch, near Petticoat lane (Middlesex Street), to a Huguenot family who had sought refuge from persecution in France. He was educated at St Paul's School and Jesus College, Cambridge before becoming a priest with posts as a parish priest and lecturer. He was mostly occupied writing about the lives and works of post-Reformation bishops and archbishops and in 1720 he compiled an updated version of John Stow's *Survey of London*.

Despite Strype's praise it was claimed by those attending the meeting at Garraway's that the Stocks Market was responsible for a muck heap behind the Royal Exchange, 'which had been untouched for a year except by additions'. The market was demolished in 1737 to make way for the present Mansion House and temporarily relocated to the vicinity of Fleet Street before disappearing from history. It is suggested by some authorities that the name was adopted by stockbrokers to describe their activities though this is not certain.

One of the principal rivals to Garraway's in what was still a very informal market was a few doors away in Exchange (now Change) Alley at Jonathan's Coffee House, opened by Jonathan Miles in 1680. In 1695 John Houghton (1645–1705), a London apothecary, left an account of life in the City at the time, giving a description of the early days of share trading:

> The manner of managing the trade is this: the monied man goes among the brokers which are chiefly upon the [Royal] Exchange and at Jonathan's Coffee House, sometimes Garraway's and at some other coffee houses and asks how stocks go and upon information bids the broker buy or sell so many shares in such and such stocks.

In 1698 a further step was taken towards the modern stock market with the publication of a bulletin entitled *The Course of the Exchange and other Things* by John Castaing which listed the prices of shares and also of

The sealing of the charter of the Bank of England, 1694. (Patent and Copyright Office, Library and Archives Canada)

commodities such as salt, coal and paper. John Castaing was of Huguenot descent with contacts amongst fellow Huguenots in the Netherlands. It was no coincidence that the bulletin was normally published on Tuesdays and Fridays, the days before the twice-weekly departure of a packet boat which sailed to the Hook of Holland, taking his bulletin for the guidance of the merchants of the Netherlands. It may be regarded as the precursor of the Stock Exchange Official List and of the pages of the *Financial Times*. Castaing wrote under the name 'John Broker' and his bulletin reflected the fact that the turnover of shares in large concerns at this time was becoming substantial. In 1704 £1.8 million of shares were traded in the Bank of England and the East India Company – about 85 per cent of the capital of the two concerns.

The Bank of England

The Bank of England had been created in 1694 to act as the banker for the British government and in particular to finance the wars waged against King Louis XIV of France. The idea was that of William Paterson, a Scot, who later devised the disastrous Darien scheme. In the event the Bank of England was successful in raising £1.2 million with an interest rate of 8 per cent, underwritten by the British government, to equip the Royal Navy for the conflict. The loan and interest were serviced by duties on shipping and beer and the bank quickly gained a reputation for reliability and probity. The activity financed by the loan, in shipbuilding and associated industries and in providing food and other supplies for the greatly enlarged Royal Navy, generated an economic boom in industry and agriculture which underpinned the government's finances and presaged the industrial development of the eighteenth century: a premature example, perhaps, of a Keynesian stimulus to the economy prompted by government expenditure. The Bank, which became central to the management of the economy and the National Debt, remained a private concern owned by its shareholders until it was nationalised in 1946. In 1998 it regained a measure of autonomy when it was given the responsibility for setting interest rates independently of the Treasury. It was the model for virtually all other Central Banks that followed it. The Bank's history since its foundation is told in its museum, which is entered from Bartholomew Lane on the eastern side of the bank itself. At present the museum is open from 10 a.m. to 5 p.m. on Fridays though it is wise to check the website in advance at: www.bankofengland.co.uk.

The Darien Scheme

This scheme, like that of the Bank of England, was promoted by William Paterson, but met only disaster. London financiers were unimpressed by the claims that untold riches were to be found in the Darien Isthmus in Central America but he persuaded his fellow Scots to invest most of the country's wealth in an expedition which found only poisonous snakes, disease and death. It effectively bankrupted Scotland and the nation's finances were restored by a payment of £400,000 from the English Treasury, the country being driven into the Acts of Union with England in 1707, which meant the loss of Scotland's Parliament for 300 years.

The Huguenots and the Jews

John Castaing (the name is sometimes spelt Costaing) was a Huguenot, one of thousands of French Protestants who left France from the late seventeenth century to escape persecution by Louis XIV. Most of the Huguenot families went to the Protestant Netherlands or Great Britain and, while many of them were impoverished silk-weavers who settled in Spitalfields, a substantial minority were prosperous merchants who established their own church in Threadneedle Street, close to the Bank of England and the coffee houses. Their Protestant religion had excluded them from the court, the professions and the military of Louis XIV's increasingly intolerant regime so, like the Quakers in England, they had gone into business and prospered. The Huguenots brought to London their experience and skills as traders and manufacturers and, above all, large sums of money seeking opportunities for investment. The size of the financial exodus may be measured by a book of 1689 by a French writer, Michel Levassor, entitled *The Sighs of France in Slavery* who wrote of the Huguenots that they took into exile, 'immense sums which have drawn dry the fountain of commerce' in France. France's loss was London's gain. When the Bank of England was founded in 1694, to fund the wars against Louis XIV, a substantial proportion of its capital was subscribed by Huguenot families who thereby helped to finance Marlborough's devastating victories over the armies of Louis, their former oppressor. They also maintained close links with their fellow emigrants in the Netherlands, Europe's other major trading nation, providing intelligence about cargoes, shipwrecks and prices that informed John Castaing's bulletins. In addition to Castaing's publications, some of the coffee houses employed boys whom they would despatch to the docks to pick up news of shipments that were arriving, or had failed to arrive; and to the homes of merchants to gather gossip from servants. News would be shown on boards in the coffee house itself or circulated on news-sheets. Huguenots were joined in the markets by other outcasts including Jewish immigrants who had been invited back to England by Oliver Cromwell during the Protectorate which followed the English Civil War and who, because of their exclusion from other professions on the Continent, had taken to banking and trade.

Thieves and Thief Takers

Some idea of the atmosphere that prevailed in Jonathan's Coffee House may be gained by reading an advertisement that appeared in the *Daily Courant* on 21 November 1720:

> Lost out of a pocket at Jonathan's Coffee House in Exchange Alley on Saturday 19th inst. a plain vellum pocket book wherein was a first subscription to the South Sea Company of £1,000 South Sea Bonds. Whoever brings the said book, with the papers therein contained, to Mr Jonathan Wilde in the Old Bailey shall have five guineas and no questions asked.

Jonathan Wilde (1683–1725) was a notorious thief taker who earned money in three ways. First, he organised robberies carried out by his numerous contacts in the criminal underworld of eighteenth-century London. He then advertised his services to victims of the crimes and was rewarded by them

The IDLE PRENTICE Executed at Tyburn.

An execution at Tyburn, *c.* 1750; note the three-legged scaffold in the background and the viewing platforms for spectators to the right. (William Hogarth)

for 'recovering' their property. Finally, as a thief taker he earned money from the authorities by giving evidence against the thieves. His unpopularity reached its peak when he was responsible for the arrest of the serial thief Jack Sheppard whose repeated escapes from Newgate prison had made him a popular hero. Sheppard's execution at Tyburn in 1724 attracted sympathetic crowds but Wilde's execution in May 1725, witnessed by a huge crowd that included Daniel Defoe, was a scene of public rejoicing. The pickpocket who stole the pocket book from Jonathan's was presumably one of Wilde's stooges, which gives an idea of the coffee house's clientele at the time.

'Loitering and gambling'

In 1698 the cause of the coffee houses was helped by the decision to ban dealers in stocks from the Royal Exchange for their 'loitering and gambling'. In 1696 Parliament was already sufficiently concerned by 'the pernicious art of stock jobbing' to institute an enquiry into the matter. At this point there was no distinction between stock*brokers*, who simply bought or sold shares on behalf of a client in return for a commission on the transaction; and stock*jobbers* who owned and traded shares on their own account. The jobbers, by acting in effect as wholesalers prepared to hold and trade in shares, added liquidity to the market since it was not then necessary for a trader who wished to sell shares to find another investor who wished to buy the same shares. But there was a temptation for a jobber to recommend to a client, for whom he was acting as broker, that the client buy shares which he, the jobber, wanted to unload. The following year an Act was passed to restrain brokers and jobbers who had 'carried on most unjust practices and designs and unlawfully combined and confederated themselves to raise or fall from time to time the value of [securities] most convenient for their own private interest and advantage'. Under the terms of the Act the number of brokers was limited to one hundred, to be registered by the Lord Mayor, under oath, each to deposit a bond to the value of £500, which would be forfeited in the event of misbehaviour. Commissions were to be limited to a maximum of 10 per cent (in later centuries it would be a fraction of 1 per cent and in some cases zero) and anyone trading without a licence would be fined £100 and spend an hour a day in the pillory for three days. The Act would apply for ten years.

Bulls, Bears, Stags, Lame Ducks and Low Wretches

In 1707 the Act expired and the number of brokers increased, as did the levels of trading and speculation, a sequence of events that was to end in disaster at the end of the following decade. In the meantime a number of creatures were to emerge which would become a permanent feature of stock market folklore. In 1714 the expressions Bulls and Bears were in common use on the exchanges and in 1761 Thomas Mortimer, whose written works include many on the subject of the wealthy and the London markets wrote in *Every Man his Own Broker* that a bear was 'a person who has agreed to sell any quantity of the public funds more than he is possessed of' adding that the bear would then hope to buy the stocks once they had fallen to a level lower than the price for which he had already agreed to sell them. Bulls on the other hand were 'all persons who buy any quantity of government securities without the intention or ability to pay for it and are consequently obliged to sell it again either at a profit or a loss before the time comes when they have agreed to pay for it'. Such people still exist. They are called hedge fund managers, speculating in stocks, which they do not intend to hold as investments. It is a sophisticated form of gambling and it doesn't always turn out well. Stags were people who subscribed for newly issued shares that they believed would rise in value before they began to be traded, the shares then being sold before they had to be paid for. This still happens. The expression Lame Duck was 'a name given in Change Alley to those who refuse to fulfil their engagements' thereby in effect making them pariahs with no future in the market. The activities of bulls and bears were facilitated by the six-week settlement period which applied in the eighteenth century and which meant that transactions entered into at the beginning of the period did not have to be settled for six weeks, giving the trader the time, if he had judged the market correctly, to make a profit without actually having to part with any capital.

By the early eighteenth century trading in stocks was attracting critical attention. As early as 1716 a critic had written of:

> the vermin called stockjobbers who prey upon, destroy and discourage all Industry and honest gain, for no sooner is any Trading company erected or any villainous project to cheat the public set up, but it is immediately divided into shares, and then traded for in Exchange Alley, before it is known whether the project has any intrinsic value.

The reputation of the jobbers did not improve with the passage of time as later in the century, in his *Dictionary* of 1755 Dr Samuel Johnson described a jobber as, 'A low wretch who gets money by buying and selling shares in the funds'. Perhaps both authors had suffered at the hands of jobbers who, despite such censure, would no doubt have been consoled by the huge sums that could be made by dealing. Jobbers could operate with the minimum of overheads and little capital. Their business was transacted on the floor of the exchange so they barely needed an office. And if they bought and sold shares within the six week settlement period they had need for minimal capital, so if a jobber read the market correctly and had nerves of iron he could make a great deal of money quite quickly. This type of trading, where the dealer never actually took possession of the securities concerned, later become known as 'dealing for time'. Sampson Gideon (1699–1762) who began to deal in 1719 with £1,500 had by 1759 turned it into a fortune of £350,000 while David Ricardo (1772–1823), the son of a Dutchman, had by 1818 amassed a fortune of half a million pounds as a jobber. Both were descendants of Jewish families who had taken to trade and banking on the Continent because their faith had excluded them from many professions. David Ricardo was frank in his assessment of the motives and sophistication of his colleagues, informing a contemporary that, although 'attentive to their business, there are very few in number who have much knowledge of political economy and consequently they pay little attention to finance as a subject of science. They consider more the immediate effect of passing events, rather than their distant consequences'. The charge of 'short termism' often levelled at the exchange is thus not new.

Trouble in the South Seas

The disaster, which duly arrived in 1720, was the South Sea Bubble, which contained many of the ingredients of twentieth-century City disasters. The South Sea Company originated in 1711 as a plan to absorb the National Debt incurred during the wars against Louis XIV. The government raised money for the wars partly through the Bank of England (see above) but also by selling lottery tickets and annuities (rights to annual payments, like pensions) in return for a lump sum. The idea was that the company would take on the annuities and lottery prizes in return for a monopoly of trade to South America, including a monopoly in slave trading. The company prospered when the War of the Spanish Succession ended with the 1713 Treaty of Utrecht. This gave trading concessions to Britain in the South American colonies of Spain, long believed to be the site of the fabulously wealthy El Dorado. It enabled the company to raise the huge sum of £2 million in shares. In addition, the collapse of the French economy caused by the wars led many financiers, including Frenchmen, to transfer their investments to London. The value of the company's shares soared, once trebling in value in a single day. They were helped by two practices that were shared by financial disasters of the twentieth century.

First, the company offered shares to wealthy individuals, including members of the government, in return for contracts, promising that when the shares increased in value the company would buy them back with its own money and allow the individuals to retain a portion of any increase in capital value: heads you win, tails you don't lose. The Guinness/Distillers takeover scandal of the 1980s had echoes of this. They also allowed small investors to buy in instalments, with a modest down payment followed by payments as the shares rose in value. This resembled the practices of the 1920s when Wall Street investors borrowed large sums to buy shares and were then unable to pay for them when their value collapsed.

Robert Walpole (1676–1745) who became Prime Minister in 1721, was amongst the few sceptics about the prospects of the South Sea Company and sold his own shares quite early in the frenzy. He was so unpopular that when he rose to speak on the subject in the House of Commons MPs who had invested in the company hurried from the chamber. Other ventures quickly followed in a speculative turmoil which saw the value of shares more than double between 1719 and 1720, with such ventures as a company devoted to creating a perpetual motion machine, one for manufacturing square cannon balls to be used against infidels and another 'for carrying on an undertaking of great advantage but nobody to know what it is'. In August 1720 the company's shares were being valued at ten times their price when launched six months earlier but the company still hadn't done any significant business. Soon rumours began to circulate that the directors who had launched the company had sold out and cashed in their profits, as indeed they had. The value of the company collapsed, the treasurer, Mr Knight, fled to France and the Chancellor of the Exchequer, who had supported the company in parliament, was sent to the Tower of London and burned in effigy.

'I can calculate the motion of heavenly bodies'

Only Robert Walpole had his reputation strengthened but it didn't make him popular, especially since he had sold his stock at a profit as the excitement mounted. There were many eminent casualties of the Bubble. Godfrey Kneller, Alexander Pope (who complained of 'an ocean of avarice and greed'), Jonathan Swift and John Gay, author of *The Beggar's Opera* were amongst them but the most notable was Sir Isaac Newton who wrote of his failed investment, 'I can calculate the motion of heavenly bodies but not the madness of people'. The South Sea Bubble was celebrated after the event in sarcastic songs, decks of playing cards, a cartoon by Hogarth and a painting of 1847 now in the Tate Gallery by Edward Matthew Ward entitled *Change Alley in the South Sea Bubble*. The episode resulted in the so-called Bubble Act of 1720, which prohibited the creation of joint stock companies without a royal charter. It remained in force until 1825. The South Sea Company's shares eventually settled at about the level at which they had begun and it survived into the nineteenth century, paying out the annuities and lottery prizes it had taken on and prospering as a trading and whaling company at South Sea House, later for a while the home of the Baltic Exchange. The company's lasting legacy is the use of the word 'bubble', to describe stock market booms when they are swiftly followed by crashes.

New Jonathan's

Chastened by this experience, a number of brokers attempted to create a more orderly market. A group of them rented Jonathan's Coffee House as an exchange and attempted to exclude those of whom they disapproved. This might have worked, however, one of those who had been barred brought a lawsuit and secured readmission. A fire that began at a wig-makers in 1748 destroyed Garraway's, Jonathan's and other coffee houses (as well as a valuable collection of butterflies) in Change Alley but the coffee houses were rebuilt. At the same time external events were increasing opportunities for trade and consequently the need to ensure that trading in securities was conducted in an orderly manner. The victorious Seven Years' War between Britain and France (1756–63) left Britain in undisputed command of India and North America and promised a huge increase in trade which, in turn, prompted a substantial increase in the number of joint stock companies and in the trading of their shares. The process was helped by the practice of banks in investing unused balances in securities, Coutts and Company (which traced its history back to 1692) being amongst the pioneers in this activity. Besides the companies involved in trade with Britain's newly acquired colonies there were shares in the rapidly expanding network of canals, the Grand Junction Canal Company, linking London with the Midlands, being at one time the largest joint-stock company in the world. As a result of all this activity a further and more successful attempt to establish a regulated exchange was made in 1773 when New Jonathan's was built in Sweeting's Alley, a thoroughfare that no longer exists, off Threadneedle Street and behind the Royal Exchange. Share dealing took place on the ground floor and a coffee room was provided upstairs, an admission fee of sixpence being charged. This became known as The Stock Exchange (the original Jonathan's having burned down for good in 1778) and may be regarded as the beginnings of the modern Stock Exchange. A blue plaque erected by the City Corporation marks the former site of Jonathan's in Change Alley.

9

The New Stock Exchange

Forbear from 'rude and trifling practices'

By 1801 the number of members had reached 500 and a larger exchange was needed. The New Exchange was built in Capel Court, just a few yards to the east of the Bank of England and adjacent to the future site of the Stock Exchange building which replaced it in 1972. The site had previously been the home of the Capel family, Earls of Essex, though the building, which was demolished to make way for the new exchange, was a boxing saloon owned by the prizefighter Daniel Mendoza (1764–1836). The new exchange was governed by the so-called Committee of Proprietors, which owned the exchange building and was elected by the members. The committee administered the rule book of the exchange, which was devised in 1812. Some hint of the behaviour which characterised the exchange and which had caused the expulsion of stockbrokers from the Royal Exchange in 1698 is given by the anxious tone of the introduction to the new rule book:

> The Committee earnestly recommend to the several members that *order and decorum* which is so essentially necessary to be observed in all places of business and that they forbear, on their own parts, and discourage as much as possible in others, those rude and trifling practices which have too long disgraced the Stock Exchange in the estimation of the public, which would not be tolerated in any other place.

The 'rude and trifling practices' were enumerated and the throwing of paper balls was singled out for criticism but, as we will observe later, these injunctions were not entirely effective and the paper balls which particularly vexed the committee were mild compared with some later excesses.

The committee (which eventually developed into the Committee for General Purposes which effectively managed the exchange) included John

The 'New' Stock Exchange, Capel Court, 1810. (Wikimedia Commons, public domain)

Capel, a descendant of the family which had originally owned the land, and David Ricardo (1772–1823) who, besides being a successful stockbroker, was to follow Adam Smith as an advocate of economic theories which promoted free trade, a philosophy which was to inform British economic policy throughout the nineteenth century and beyond. New members had to be sponsored by three existing members, each of whom pledged £300 (a sum which varied as the century moved on) as a surety. Those who were successful in gaining such sponsorship then had to be elected by ballot of existing members, with some preference being given to applicants who had previously worked as clerks to members and were familiar with the exchange's procedures. Only members were admitted to the trading floor and, in the words of a contemporary account, 'A stranger is soon detected, and by the custom of the place is made to understand that he is an intruder, and turned out'. Such turning out could be humiliating since, 'he was sure to be hustled, find lighted squibs put into his pocket, or his hat and wig canted out before him' according to one commentator. Members, who paid an annual fee to cover the expenses of running the building, had to be re-elected every year and bankrupts immediately forfeited membership. By the time that the above account was written, in 1850, commission had fallen to a fraction of 1 per cent. No minimum commission rates were set until the twentieth century though in September 1813 a broker called Luke Leake was censured for luring away the client of another broker with a promise of a lower commission rate than the normal one eighth of 1 per cent.

Skulduggery: the 'death' of Napoleon

These measures, designed to ensure that dealing in shares was conducted with honesty and competence, did not prevent outright fraud. In 1814 a mysterious man dressed in a military uniform and claiming to be a Colonel de Bourg and aide-de-camp to the British ambassador to Russia, announced that Napoleon had been killed by Cossacks in Russia. This prompted a rapid rise in share prices and especially in the price of a British government stock called Omnium. When the story was shown to be false the price fell again but in the meantime several stockholders had disposed of their holdings at a substantial profit. In the twentieth century this became known as 'Creating a false market in shares'. Suspicion fell upon a group of six, of whom one was the naval hero and Scottish aristocrat Thomas Cochrane, Earl of Dundonald (1775–1860) who was feared by the French as much as Nelson had been. Cochrane had disposed of £139,000 of Omnium stock that he had purchased only a month earlier and it was suggested that the mysterious 'Colonel de Bourg' had been seen entering Cochrane's house. Cochrane and others were found guilty of the fraud after a long and controversial trial. Cochrane was ordered to pay a fine of £1,000 and sentenced to stand in the pillory though this order was later revoked for fear of causing a riot in support of the popular naval hero. He was also stripped of his knighthood but a long campaign to secure his pardon was eventually successful and his knighthood was restored by a sympathetic Queen Victoria. In 1876 Cochrane's grandson was paid £40,000 by the government in compensation for his ancestor's humiliation.

More Members, More Opportunities

The increase in the membership of the exchange that occurred during the wars reflected the growing availability and diversity of investment opportunities. Securities traded on the Stock Exchange can be shares, which give the owner a share in the ownership of a company, a vote in the governance of its affairs, a share of its profits in the form of dividends and the opportunity to make a capital gain when the shares increase in value. Shares are often referred to as equity. Alternatively, securities can be bonds, which are in effect a loan to a company that earns interest but not a share in its profits or its governance. Bonds may increase in value as a company prospers (making the bond a safer loan) or decrease if a company falters and there is a danger that it will default on the loan. Governments also issue securities, usually in the form of bonds (forming much of the National Debt), which carry interest, are traded on stock markets and fluctuate in value according to the reputation of the government and the ease with which it raises money. Such government bonds are sometimes referred to as gilts or gilt-edged securities because they are regarded as very unlikely to default. The Euro crisis of 2012 was characterised by the fact that certain EU governments whose finances were regarded as shaky were having to pay higher rates of interest on their loans than they could afford because of a perception that they might default on them. Flotations of companies on the market normally involve making shares available to the public though they may involve bonds. Occasionally, flotations do not involve raising capital at all but are undertaken to establishing the value of its shares in the market, thereby enabling the owners to withdraw some of their capital at a realistic value.

New Securities, Rooks and Pigeons

The exchange had also benefited from the wars when, in 1795, Napoleon's army occupied Amsterdam which was London's principal trading rival. Several Dutch dealers fled to London, including Samuel de Zoete who founded one of the City's most successful firms of brokers. In the years following the

Napoleonic Wars, the exchange benefited from two further developments that proceeded from the wars. The first was the increase in government debt, which had grown from £456 million in 1801 to £844 million by 1819. In the later words of Disraeli, the Prime Minister William Pitt the Younger, 'caught them in the alleys of Lombard Street and clutched them from the counting houses of Cornhill'. The debt was accounted for by gilt-edged securities, which were actively traded on the floor of the new exchange. In addition, there arose a market in foreign securities, including those of foreign governments, which became so active that a room on the ground floor of Capel Court was devoted to this market on 1 January 1823. At the same time the number of members of the exchange grew, from 498 in 1802 to 804 by 1826 and a number of partnerships began to appear which would endure, with names like James Capel and Cazenove, the latter family being of Huguenot descent. Others, however, were more fleeting and a number of failures of brokers and jobbers aroused the disapproval of contemporary commentators who began to see the exchange as little more than a gambling den, leading to doggerel of the kind that appeared in a satirical work of 1819 entitled *The Financial House that Jack Built*.

These are the rooks
That prey on the pigeons
That flock around the House
That Jack built.

Rooks were jobbers, pigeons speculators and the House was the exchange in Capel Court.

An Anxious Interlude

On Monday, 10 April, 1848, some anxious hours passed in the Stock Exchange as the last of the great Chartist demonstrations, having gathered on Kennington Common, made its way in a procession about 12,000 strong through the City. The Chartists were calling for parliamentary reforms but poverty and unemployment were amongst their complaints and the Bank of England and the Stock Exchange were possible targets for their grievances. The Mansion House, the Royal Exchange and the Bank of England were guarded by troops and many members of the Stock Exchange itself were sworn in as special constables. It was proposed that the Stock Exchange be closed but it was felt that this would send out a message of panic. However, trading was subdued until, at about 2 p.m., the news was received that the Chartists had made their way back to Kennington Common and dispersed peacefully, at which point members removed their hats, sang 'God save the Queen' and the value of government stock 'immediately went up'. The following day the *Morning Chronicle* reported 'the triumph of order over the mob, the victory of peace and order against violence and intimidation'. It should be noted that the mild Chartist demonstration had been preceded by more violent upheavals in Sicily, France, several German states and Denmark so a degree of anxiety in 1848, the 'Year of Revolutions' was in order and London escaped lightly.

The Railway Bubble

The repeal of the Bubble Act in 1825 made it easier to create joint stock companies and this measure, together with the industrial boom of the nineteenth century, led to a huge increase in the volume of business, with trading in the shares of railways becoming so great that some of it intruded on the room supposedly devoted to foreign securities, to the irritation of its official occupants. Exchanges also sprang up in industrial towns like Liverpool and Manchester, both in 1836, where railways had transformed the economy. Those in Liverpool and Manchester survived well into the twentieth century though others, in towns like Dundee and Cardiff, were more short-lived. Speculation in railway shares comparable to that of the South Sea Bubble followed, often on the flimsiest of evidence. The most infamous was the Railway Mania of the 1840s when, following the successful opening in 1830 of the Liverpool to Manchester Railway which earned Stephenson's *Rocket* a place in history, a network of railways spread swiftly across the country so that by 1840 many of the key population and industrial centres had been linked. This did not deter hopeful investors from supporting less viable schemes including some which were unrealistic (such as building railways in dead straight lines regardless of geography and land ownership) and some that were fraudulent. Since many of the investors were Members of Parliament the promoters had no difficulty obtaining the necessary Acts and at the height of the mania, in 1846, 272 Acts were passed. The boom was briefly sustained by railway magnates like George Hudson, 'the Railway King' (1800–71), paying dividends out of new capital. However, when doubts began to surface share prices collapsed and, although a few viable lines emerged, notably in North-Eastern England, many investors lost their savings resulting in at least one suicide. One is reminded of the dot.com boom of the 1990s. George Hudson, who had been an early collaborator of George Stephenson on sound railway schemes, was found to have bribed MPs to support his schemes and was disgraced though he remained as MP for Sunderland. He left his grand house situated at Albert Gate, to the south of Hyde Park in London (then the tallest private residence in London, now the French Embassy) and lived the remainder of his life mostly on the Continent after a spell in a debtors' prison in York.

New Investors, New Investments

In the second half of the nineteenth century the business of the exchange grew rapidly and changed in character. In 1854, to accommodate the growing membership, which was approaching 1,000, the exchange was rebuilt on a grander scale to give a trading area twice as large. Between 1850 and 1913, a time of peace, the national debt actually fell from £775 million to £593 million, reducing the scope for investment in government gilts, while the economy more than quadrupled in size. Insurance companies and banks therefore began to seek investment opportunities in securities other than land and government debt. Other openings soon presented themselves. Such investments had amounted to little more than £25 million in 1870 and had reached more than £250 million by 1913. The Investment Trust was an innovation of the 1860s, a company which, rather than making or selling anything, simply invested in the shares of other companies, thus spreading risk and, in effect, placing the services of a fund manager at the disposal of smaller investors. The first major investment trust, launched in 1868, was Foreign and Colonial whose name indicates the nature of its investments. It continues to thrive, one of the largest trusts quoted on the exchange of the twenty-first century. Companies included railways and docks (British and foreign, especially the rapidly expanding United States networks); foreign government debt; and industrial companies in Britain, North America and the Empire, especially in the production of raw materials and foodstuffs like coal, metals, rubber and tea. In an era of free trade, raw materials were imported from the British Empire, the United States and South America while manufactured goods, notably textiles and machinery, were exported, each development in trade offering opportunities for investment and trading in shares. In principle, however, the exchange would list any joint-stock company whose shares were likely to generate sufficient turnover to earn commissions for brokers, a notable example being the Guinness Company, which issued shares to the public in 1886, raising £6 million through the flotation, which was managed by Barings. At the same time the number of foreign members of the exchange increased rapidly, with brokers from Germany joining those from colonies like Australia and Malaya that were producing the raw materials and manufactured goods that were of interest to the dealers. Germans also became prominent in the merchant banking community with Alexander Kleinwort, the Schroder brothers and later Sigmund Warburg founding banks in London, as had the German Baring brothers in 1762.

Barings

Barings was founded in 1762 by John and Francis Baring, brothers of German descent, made its name in the raising of loans for foreign governments and enterprises, a particular triumph being the raising of 315 million francs (£12 million pounds) for the French government which took office after the fall of Napoleon. The Duke of Wellington commented that Barings had 'to a certain degree the command of the money market of the world' while the Duc de Richelieu added, 'There are six great powers in Europe: England, France, Prussia, Austria, Russia and Baring brothers.' Later in the century Barings' success in flotations of companies like Guinness led to their making a number of unwise loans to South America which brought the bank to the brink of ruin when Argentina defaulted on its loans. It was rescued by the Bank of England with financial support from Rothschilds. No such rescue was available in 1995 when unwise investments in the Far East by a trader in Singapore, Nick Leeson, led to the failure and disappearance of the world's oldest merchant bank.

Merchant Banks

Merchant banks and Investment banks like Rothschilds are critical to the creation of new joint stock companies and the expansion of existing ones. They arose in the Middle Ages when Jewish traders, who were unaffected by the usury laws which forbade Christians to lend money for interest, loaned money to merchants who were despatching ships on long voyages. They had excellent prospects for profits (from trading spices for example) but a long delay would ensue before profits could be realised: hence the need for medium term finance. Following the Reformation of the sixteenth century the usury laws no longer applied and by the eighteenth century banks like Barings were involved in extensive international investments. Other banks soon followed. Their activities later extended to raising capital from contacts in the markets such as investment trusts and pension fund managers who were looking for sound investments either in new companies or in new shares in expanding companies. When a company's shares are first offered for sale the company's sponsor, often a stockbroker or bank, will estimate the price at which the shares should be offered for sale and then seek an underwriting pool, a group of investors who will in effect underwrite the price of the offer by agreeing to purchase any unsold shares at the agreed price. The lead underwriter who co-ordinates the offer and signs up enough investors is sometimes referred to as the bookrunner. The underwriters will receive a fee and if the offering is successful and all the shares taken up the underwriters will not have to buy any stock. The expression merchant bank is now rarely used, investment bank being preferred since the Big Bang of 1986 when such banks expanded their activities into trading shares on their own account, a potentially more profitable but also riskier activity as Barings discovered when its trading in markets its managers didn't fully understand led to its collapse.

The London market also gained a reputation at this time, in contrast to later judgements, for making long-term investments in new and by implication risky ventures. Cazenove handled no fewer than fifty new company flotations between 1884 and 1914 and at this time the London market was the source of finance for the oil industry, a giant of the future but at the time a much less certain prospect, while it was in London that the Wireless Telegraph and Signal Company was floated in 1897. Later known as Marconi, it followed swiftly upon the Italian inventor's demonstration of the practicality of wireless transmission though at the time its prospects looked much more hazardous than they did a few years later. The spirit of enterprise and risk-taking was very much alive on the exchange at the turn of the nineteenth and twentieth centuries though it should be added that the process by which companies were floated was very far from sophisticated. The *Investor's Monthly Manual* described the process in 1910:

> Much of the present-day underwriting is done on the Stock Exchange, and a member will approach another with sometimes little more than a slip of paper, upon which are jotted particulars of the people connected with the matter, the proposed capital, profit estimates etc ... The names on the paper are what really count, and if first-class people are connected with any concern, underwriting will present no difficulties.

How different would it be now?

'So bad an example'

The introduction of foreign members of the exchange did nothing to improve the behaviour about which the committee had been so anxious and insistent when it drew up the rules in 1812. In June 1851 the managers of the exchange called upon the General Purposes Committee to do something about 'the disgraceful scene which occurred in the Exchange yesterday afternoon, a football having been introduced and between one and two hundred members engaged in the play for a considerable time'. The committee identified one Henry Brown as amongst the culprits responsible for conduct 'derogatory to the character of the Exchange' and expressed particular distress that Henry, a son of one of the committee, 'should set so bad an example to the junior members of the House'. Mr Brown's penitence was severely qualified since he feared that if he gave an 'absolute pledge' concerning his future conduct 'on the impulse of the moment he might be led away to forget it but he said he would endeavour to control any such impetuosity and restrain himself as much as possible and avoid play for the future.' Hardly a resounding apology!

Competition and Specialisation, but No Advertising

Such was the volume of trading in raw materials that in 1909 the Mincing Lane Tea and Rubber Brokers' Association was set up on the later site of Plantation House to deal in plantation products whose volatility in price made them unattractive, though the business of this and other similar exchanges trading in mining shares was soon absorbed by the Stock Exchange. Other forms of competition emerged. Nottingham and Huddersfield were amongst the towns which produced their own (albeit short-lived) exchanges at this time, specialising in local industries like lace and woollen textiles and the *Daily Mail*, under its resolute and imaginative proprietor Alfred Harmsworth, Lord Northcliffe (1865–1922), began to advertise shares for sale in its columns in order to match buyers and sellers without the need for the intervention of a stockbroker and his commission. By 1884 the exchange had 2,574 members and by 1905 this had more than doubled to 5,567. At the same time the growing competition and the diversity of the business was reflected in a degree of specialisation amongst its members. One of those who joined the exchange at this time, with a knowledge of the rubber market, after a career in the Far East, was Henry Panmure Gordon (1837–1902). The jobbing firm of Durlacher, formed in 1881, began by specialising in railway shares and moved into brewing. Both Panmure Gordon and Durlacher are names that have survived into the twenty-first century. At the same time some brokers began to specialise. James Capel focused on the investment needs of banks like Coutts and Drummonds while Cazenove dealt with Barings and Rothschilds. Members of the exchange were forbidden to advertise their services but evaded this prohibition by paying commissions to lawyers, doctors and bankers who were advising their clients. The prohibition on jobbers also being brokers was also widely ignored despite changes in the code in 1847, 1877 and 1903 and the division was not made effective until a new rule was passed in 1909 specifically outlawing the practice.

The Rothschild Banking Dynasty

Nathan Rothschild (1777–1836) was one of five sons of Mayer Rothschild, founder of the banking dynasty of that name. Mayer despatched
his sons to the five major commercial centres of Europe, sending
Nathan to Manchester to manage the family's textile business. Nathan,
who became a British citizen, moved to London where he founded the
Rothschild bank and dealt in gold bullion and securities, specialising
in those of foreign governments. His Rothschild colleagues on the
continent provided him with information that enabled him accurately
to assess their value, to his advantage. Such contacts brought him the
news of Wellington's victory at Waterloo a day ahead of the government's official messengers. He played a major part in raising money
to finance the war against Napoleon and helped finance the British
government's abolition of slavery by raising a loan to buy out the plantation owners. The Rothschilds were a cornerstone of British banking
and government finance in the nineteenth century and in 1875, when
Disraeli decided to purchase shares in the Suez Canal, he turned not to
Parliament but to Nathan's son Lionel (1808–79) because, as Disraeli
explained to the Prince of Wales of the Rothschilds, 'They alone could
have accomplished what we wanted and they had only twenty-four
hours to make up their minds whether they would, or could, incur an
immediate liability of £4 million'. In 1858 Lionel entered the House of
Commons, the first Jewish Member of Parliament, after being refused
admission on several previous occasions because of his refusal to take
the Christian oath. The Rothschild bank continues to trade from New
Court, EC4, where Nathan began in 1804. Until 2004 the twice-daily
conference fixing the price of gold, a price recognised throughout
the world, took place in Rothschilds' offices. In that year Rothschilds
withdrew from gold trading and the conference is now conducted by
telephone by the market participants.

New Technologies and New Markets

Later in the century the first tentative steps were taken to introduce new
technologies, the first move in the direction of developments that, the following century, would transform the business of the exchange. In 1868, following
the invention of the ticker-tape machine the previous year, the Exchange
Telegraph Company sought permission to install one of its machines on the
floor of the exchange to collect and transmit prices. The proprietors of the
exchange refused permission, explaining that, 'they had no guarantee but that
prices might be wired to other places than the offices of brokers, and might

tend to the formation of markets elsewhere'. The proprietors of the exchange, whose profits and dividends were earned by the membership fees paid by the brokers (ten guineas a year and rising) wished to maintain their grip on securities trading and to prevent other markets from developing outside its walls. However, pressure from the members/brokers ensured that the first ticker-tape machine was hesitantly introduced in 1872, enabling share prices and other news to be transmitted from international markets and shortly afterwards, with equal misgivings, the exchange received its first telephone. Submarine cables to France (1851) and New York (1866) meant that prices in these markets could be known in London within twenty minutes of their being quoted and such was the interest in New York stocks that dealings in its shares began as soon as the market opened (at 3 p.m. London time) and continued in surrounding streets when the London Exchange closed at 4 p.m. These changes in communications created a new market that attracted jobbers who were interested in turning a quick profit, albeit on small margins. This was the market for international arbitrage, which exploited the small differences in the quoted prices of securities that were often found in different markets and was defined by the exchange itself as:

> The business of buying and selling a security as a principal in one centre, with the intention of reversing such transaction in a centre in a country different from that in which the original transaction has taken place, in order to profit from the price difference between such centres.

Such transactions could only take place when information about such price differences was swiftly available and could instantly be exploited. In the nineteenth century it was a small part of the exchange's business but by 1909 telegrams were being exchanged between London and continental exchanges every three seconds of the working day and with New York every six seconds. Following the Big Bang of 1986 with trading occurring on computer screens, it became a substantial proportion of the transactions, accounting for much of the frantic shouting in dealing rooms as dealers hastened to exploit such differences in prices before competitors could do so, thereby earning a profit which, though on a small margin, was virtually free of risk.

'A low class of members'

A Royal Commission of 1878 was prompted by a bout of speculative frenzy that gave rise to complaints in parliament that the exchange had, 'encouraged speculation by admitting a low class of members with small security'. A number of promoters had persuaded investors to participate in loans to

Honduras, Costa Rica and Paraguay, which plunged in value. At this time the regulations governing the promotion of companies were so lax as to encourage confidence tricksters to persuade gullible investors to part with their money and this gave the markets a poor reputation. One of the most active and ruthless company promoters was 'Baron' Albert Grant (1830–99). Born Abraham Gottheimer in Dublin he changed his name to Albert Grant and was an early exponent of the black art of direct mailing. He obtained names and addresses of widows, clergymen and other small investors and persuaded them, with lavish promises of returns, to invest in such enterprises as the Cadiz Waterworks, the Imperial Bank of China, the Labuan Coal Company and the Emma Silver Mine, the last two supposedly in South America which continued to be regarded by many as an El Dorado. In his lifetime he raised £24 million from hopeful investors of which £20 million was lost, none of it his. In 1873 he spent some of this ill-gotten fortune on a 'Bachelors' Ball' at his huge house near Kensington which was seized by angry creditors who demolished it, sold the land and sold the main staircase to Madame Tussauds. After being made a 'hereditary baron of the Kingdom of Italy' for services to the new kingdom in developing a shopping centre in Milan, he styled himself 'Baron Grant'. Following several lawsuits against him he died in penury in 1899, his obituary notice in the *Illustrated London News* recording that he was 'a man of agreeable presence and enthusiastic manners whose death brought back to mind many an ancient adventure of his as company promoter, mine owner, millionaire and bankrupt'. Such were the men whose schemes the Stock Exchange of the 1870s accommodated and who inspired Anthony Trollope's contemporary novel *The Way We Live Now* with its crooked financier Augustus Melmotte who, like Albert Grant, was of Jewish descent and born overseas. Such men also inspired a pamphlet which appeared at the time and spoke of the precarious social standing of 'the stockbroker, whose social position is so sudden that it cannot yet be looked upon as assured, whose wealth, though great, has the garish hue of luck and the glories associated with it which may at any moment dissolve into thin air'.

Discreditable Rumours

In the circumstances it is not surprising that discreditable rumours about stockbrokers spread quickly. On Christmas Eve, 1874, there was a railway accident involving a Great Western train at Shipton-on-Cherwell near Oxford in which thirty people died and many more were injured. Amidst the carnage there were reports, carried in *The Times*, of acts of individual bravery as 'the more slightly injured at once set to work with praiseworthy alacrity to help their distressed fellow travellers' but a story soon emerged that not all had behaved nobly. It was claimed that an unnamed stockbroker, emerging unscathed from the wreckage, had swiftly made his way to the nearest telegraph office and wired his clerk to sell his Great Western shares. True or not, such stories reflected the low esteem into which the market had fallen. Nevertheless the Royal Commission which enquired into the exchange concluded that it was run in an honest and orderly manner, in a way 'salutary to the public interests', in the words of the son of Charles Dickens who wrote an account of the exchange's work in 1879.

'Is the Stock Exchange rotten?'

As one scandal or abuse receded, another arose. In 1898 the influential *Investors' Review* ran an article entitled 'Is the Stock Exchange rotten?' which argued that cliques were profiting from privileged access to sensitive information, a process which would later be known as insider trading; and from the manipulation of share values by groups of investors, as Cochrane had allegedly done, later known as a concert party. Much of the criticism was levelled at the press, with allegations that editors and journalists had received payments in return for recommending or 'pushing' shares. Harry Marks, the founder-editor of *Financial News* was alleged to have received £31,110, a huge sum for the time, much of it being paid for suppressing unfavourable comments on a share issue. Of this £25,000 was paid by a company promoter called Ernest Hooley who, in 1898, was found to have made between £100,000 and £200,000 by promoting twenty-six companies of which almost all were struggling or bankrupt. When asked by the London Bankruptcy Court why he had paid so much money to Marks, Hooley explained, to general laughter, that it was because Mrs Marks was a friend. Even the *Financial Times* was not above suspicion. Founded in 1888 with the promise that it was for 'The Honest Financier and the Respectable Broker', its editor Douglas Macrae had evidently received £2,000 from Hooley though Hooley added, to further laughter, that Macrae was 'The honestest man of the lot'.

'The only really international market'

In the late nineteenth century the number of members of the Stock Exchange increased rapidly, much of the increase being due to the way in which it was owned and organised. The building was owned by its shareholders who had every reason to encourage new members to join since their subscription fees, which rose steadily from ten guineas to forty guineas a year by the end of the century, were the principal source of income. The members, on the other hand, preferred to restrict membership in order to reduce competition and protect their commissions. In 1904 a campaign began to limit the membership, led by a stockbroker with the unforgettable name of Ferdinand Faithfull Begg who was also a Member of Parliament noted for his loquaciousness and for the number of letters of complaint that he wrote to newspapers. It was written of him that, 'nobody is anxious to hear his opinions a second time' but he was pushing at an open door and his supporters gained a majority on the General Purposes Committee. Any applicant for membership would henceforth have to purchase three shares in the exchange and secure the nomination of a retiring member. By 1905 the number of brokers had peaked at 5,567, falling to 4,855 by 1914 while the proportion of members who owned shares grew from 25 per cent to almost 50 per cent in the same period, thus bringing closer the interests of owners and members. Not until 1947, however, did the members buy out the shareholders and take full control of the exchange. In 1908, in an attempt to protect profit margins in the face of increasing competition, a rule was introduced to impose minimum commission levels though, to prevent possible abuses of the kind that had first caused anxiety in the seventeenth century, the roles of broker and jobber were separated. There was still no need for qualifications beyond the support of three existing members. Not until 1971 were new members required to pass examinations but by 1903 the London Stock Exchange was so dominant that the French ambassador wrote in a despatch that:

So close to France, the London market attracts more and more of our capital and gives the Paris Stock Exchange ever increasing competition. Many of our stockbrokers and credit companies have either correspondents or offices in London and they say that it is through their English broking that they make the greatest profit.

These views were echoed in the USA. In 1911 the activities of the London Exchange were such that a New Yorker could write that, 'The London Stock Exchange is the only really international market of the world. Its interests branch over all parts of our globe'.

The exchange had by this time developed its own slang, comparable with that of cockney rhyming slang which had also arisen in the nineteenth century as a means of enabling traders (especially barrow boys with whom stockbrokers were often compared) to communicate with one another without others, like policemen or market inspectors, understanding what they were saying. Thus Ducks were shares in the Aylesbury Dairy Company while Matches referred to Bryant and May. A turn was a profit margin on a deal, a squirt was a broker who did not deal fairly and a sweater was someone who poached business by undercutting commission rates. The cry of Fourteen Hundred indicated that a stranger (i.e. a non-member) had entered the trading floor whereupon he would be unceremoniously expelled. This referred to a mythical notion that the number of members of the exchange was limited to 1,400, so any trader who wished to be able to deal on the exchange floor and qualify for a full partnership with his broking firm would have to purchase membership (referred to as a 'nomination') from a retiring member, the price varying according to the fortunes of the exchange at the time. In fact the membership, having peaked at 5,567 in 1905, was capped at about 4,000 between the wars, standing at 4,076 in 1939. The rule remained in force until the 1970s.

10

The Stock Exchange at War

War was not new to the markets. They had profited from the Wars of the Spanish Succession in the early eighteenth century and from the Napoleonic Wars when they had helped the government to raise large sums to prosecute the campaigns. The wars of the twentieth century would present their own opportunities but would also undermine Britain's position at the centre of world trade and sterling as the prime currency for settling international debts. These factors, together with restrictions on entry operated by the 'gentlemen's club' outlook of the Stock Exchange itself, helped to weaken the City's position as an international financial centre, leading to a slow but relentless decline which would only be reversed in 1986, with the changes wrought by the so-called Big Bang which opened up the gentlemen's club to the world of international competition.

The Boer War

The attitude of the Stock Exchange towards the Boer War was ambivalent. The discovery of gold on the Witwatersrand in 1886, in an area with many distrustful settlers of Dutch descent, produced much speculative excitement which became known in the press as 'The Kaffir circus' though many commentators remained cautious about promises of untold riches in distant places that were reminiscent of El Dorado, the South Sea Company, Albert Grant and his like. The Economist described mining shares as, 'the happy hunting grounds of organised gangs of promoters who, together with their associates – low class advertising agents etc. – care nothing about the value of a mine, provided only that it can be made a means of fleecing the public'. Or, as others put it, 'A mine is a hole in the ground owned by a liar'. A turning point came in 1887 with the successful flotation of Cecil Rhodes's Gold Fields of South Africa (later Consolidated Gold Fields) by Rothschilds who had turned down

Guinness's approaches the previous year and no doubt regretted doing so. Rothschilds later oversaw the merger of Rhodes's business with other concerns to create De Beers, under the control of Rhodes.

The possibility of disorder in the gold and diamond fields which, by 1899, were clearly a sound prospect under Rhodes's ruthless management, was unwelcome and many commentators suggested that the war was fought to preserve Britain's access to the gold fields with their steady supply of bullion for the nation's reserves. The economist J.A. Hobson, a persistent critic of imperialism, claimed that the Boer War was, 'The clearest and most dramatic instance of the operation of the world-wide forces of international finance'. Not many agreed with him though; Rhodes and his colleagues were treated with great suspicion even by those who profited from their activities. The High Commissioner, Alfred Milner, conceded that it involved fighting 'for people whom we despise' but argued that the conflict was necessary to establish that the British Empire would not be frustrated by Dutch settlers.

Certainly the fortunes of war were reflected on the exchange. It benefited from the loans raised to finance the war but in early 1900 a series of reverses was reflected in low levels of activity and falling prices. However, the relief of Ladysmith in March followed by that of Mafeking in May led to wild celebrations in the exchange and the singing of 'God Save the Queen', 'Rule Britannia' and, in honour of Robert Baden-Powell the hero of Mafeking, 'For he's a jolly good fellow'. The end of the war was welcomed, especially by King Edward VII who wrote to his financial adviser, Sir Ernest Cassel, 'You will have doubtless heard that Peace is signed … Consols are sure to go up tomorrow. Could you not make a large investment for me?' Consols were a type of government debt, also known as 'gilts'. Clearly the king was a shrewd investor.

The First World War

Although international tension and hostility had been evident for many years before 1914 the approach of the First World War at the end of July that year caught the nation, and the City, unprepared. The financial journalist Hartley Withers (1867–1950) recorded that 'It came upon us like a thunderbolt from a clear blue sky', a situation made more awkward by the fact that, of the 218 members of the exchange who were of foreign birth, 153 were from Germany and a further 20 from its ally Austria. On 31 July, the day before the declaration of war, the exchange closed, together with those of Paris, Berlin and New York. The fear was that obstacles to transferring funds because of the outbreak of war would make it impossible to complete some contracts, leading to defaults by dealers who were exposed to international deals and to panics which could cause a collapse in prices of shares and, particularly, of some government bonds. The exchange remained closed until 31 December during which time seventeen firms failed. The vacuum was partly filled by Knight, Frank and Rutley, better known as estate agents, who revived Garraway's practice of auctioning securities while the *Daily Mail*, enterprising as ever, resumed the practice of advertising its readers' shares for sale. The greatest fear was that if the exchange reopened and asset prices collapsed, many banks whose loans were secured against the value of those assets would themselves fail, making it impossible for account holders to access their deposits. The authorities were also anxious to ensure that holdings by foreigners, particularly German and Austrian nationals, could not be sold by their owners in case the proceeds were used to finance their war effort. The Treasury therefore agreed to the reopening of the exchange on a number of conditions. First, a moratorium was placed on bank loans and at the same time a minimum price was imposed on assets, beneath which no transactions could take place, thus artificially maintaining prices that were sufficient to underpin bank loans. Secondly, foreign investors were prohibited from selling any of their holdings in London, even if that was the only market for their securities. Arbitrage was forbidden and assets were to be traded for cash, with no settlement period of the kind that had allowed speculators to thrive. In these very unusual and anti-competitive conditions the exchange reopened for business on 4 January 1915.

These restrictions were administered by the General Purposes Committee of the exchange and under its guidance they were gradually relaxed as bank loans were repaid, the danger of bank defaults receded and as the government came to the markets for War Loans to finance the conflict. In August 1916 the Chancellor of the Exchequer, Reginald McKenna, congratulated the exchange on 'the admirable way in which the Stock Exchange Committee has carried out its very difficult task of administering the restrictions which have been necessitated by the war'. The lessons were not lost on the members of the exchange or those of them who served on the committee. The pre-war regulatory regime's 'light touch' meant that many 'rules' such as minimum commissions and the distinction between brokers and jobbers were more often honoured in the breach than the observance so at the end of August 1916, the Subcommittee on Rules and Regulations was asked 'to consider and report on the principles on which Stock Exchange procedure should be altered on the resumption of normal business'.

German Heard in the Stock Exchange

There was, of course, a substantial fall in the volume of business transacted and this was matched by a fall in the number of people employed. At the outbreak of war the membership numbered 4,855 and by 1918 had fallen to 3,884, the number of clerks falling from 2,327 to 1,685. Many of these had volunteered to serve in the military and had joined the Stock Exchange battalion of the Royal Fusiliers. Of approximately 1,600 members who joined, 400 were killed, a high rate of attrition even for that dreadful conflict. As with the Baltic Exchange, difficulties arose over members with German connections. When war was declared the exchange ruled that only members born in the UK or naturalised could enter the building but this left many of German parentage who were born in the UK and others born abroad who had taken British nationality. In April 1915 one member complained that he was concerned about 'the amount of German we have heard in the Stock Exchange and I should like to make the suggestion that no language but English be heard upon the floor of the House'. This was at a time when Dachshunds were being kicked off the pavement and families with names like Schmidt, who had lived in Britain for centuries, had their windows smashed so it is to the credit of the exchange that German continued to be spoken and those of German parentage continued to trade. However, anti-German feeling after the sinking of the *Lusitania* in May 1915 meant that some failed to be re-admitted to the exchange in the annual re-elections. These measures did nothing to strengthen the expertise of the exchange which was further weakened by the Treasury's insistence that absolute priority be given to the government's need to raise money to finance the war. In February 1915 Lord Reading (former barrister Rufus Isaacs and future Viceroy of India) informed the exchange on behalf of the government that, 'the question of the advisability of new issues [of company shares] from the National point of view must rest with the Treasury and not with the Stock Exchange'. In 1913, the year before the outbreak of war, the value of the National Debt accounted for 9 per cent of

The Stock Exchange's coat of arms with its motto '*Dictum Meum Pactum*' – 'My Word is My Bond'. (Kaihsu Tai)

the value of the securities quoted on the London Stock Exchange. By 1920, following the massive war loans raised during the conflict, the severe shortage of new issues and the decline in value of many stocks, the National Debt amounted to 33 per cent of the securities quoted and assumed proportionate importance in the trading on the exchange. In 1923 the exchange adopted its coat of arms and its motto *Dictum Meum Pactum*, 'My Word is My Bond'. This reflected the fact that the face-to-face trading and handshake which characterised dealing on the floor of the exchange depended upon trust rather than upon written records of transactions though cynics have been known to add the words *Whenum Suitem* to this noble phrase!

The Wall Street Crash

During the First World War the United States, for the first time in its history, had involved itself directly in the affairs of Europe while its long absence from the conflict had left it as the world's leading creditor. This had implications for the New York and London markets which had to be worked out. It meant that the Wall Street Crash of October 1929, which resulted from debt-laden speculation in shares, had a greater effect in Europe than would have been the case twenty years earlier. Ageing industries in America and Europe were sent into precipitate decline. In Great Britain the real hardship was mostly felt in areas dependent upon industries like coal mining and shipbuilding while others prospered and there was in fact a boom in house building in London and the South where newer industries prospered. Nevertheless criticism was attached to the plutocrats and market speculators of the City whom many blamed, with little reason, for the failures of industrial and economic policy by politicians who didn't understand how to manage an economy. John Maynard Keynes's time had not yet come.

John Maynard Keynes (1883–1946)

Keynes was educated at Eton and King's College Cambridge where he studied mathematics (not economics). Drawn to economics by the Cambridge economist Alfred Marshall, Keynes joined the civil service and became an adviser to Lloyd George at the Versailles peace conference that followed the First World War. Alarmed by the impossible economic terms inflicted on Germany at the conference he wrote a polemic, *The Economic Consequences of the Peace* which forecast disaster and followed this by *The Economic Consequences of Mr Churchill* which criticised the Chancellor of the Exchequer for returning sterling to the gold standard at a level which over-valued the pound and priced British exports out of many markets, helping to create the depression of the 1930s. In 1934 he produced his highly influential *A General Theory of Employment, Interest and Money* which explained how governments could manage an economy by borrowing surplus savings during recessions and spending them to create jobs and growth. He was also a great patron of the arts and founded the Arts Council. His economic views remain the subject of debate, not least during our present troubles.

'Herr Hitler is likely to prove in the interests of peace'

During the 1930s the rise of fascism on the Continent was viewed with a blend of complacency and mild approval. When Hitler, contrary to international agreements, reoccupied the Rhineland in March 1936 the view of the exchange was that 'the action of Herr Hitler is likely to prove in the interests of peace rather than of war' while the view of the stockbrokers Mathesons on the situation in Spain was that 'In Spain we have a fight between Communism and Stability', the 'stability' being otherwise known as fascism. Kleinworts actually helped one of Franco's leading supporters to gather bullion to pay for help from the Italian fascist leader Mussolini. Later the same year the market boomed in strange circumstances. Anxiety over the prospect of Edward VIII's abdication over his affair with Wallis Simpson caused the market to weaken but as soon as he announced his decision to abdicate the markets rose. Lionel Rothschild was quoted as saying, 'If anyone had said years ago that a King of England had abdicated and on the same afternoon there had been a boom on the Stock Exchange he would have been qualified for a lunatic asylum'.

'Peace with Honour'

As the situation in Europe darkened further, the news of Chamberlain's trip to Munich in September 1938 was greeted with enthusiasm, the Prime Minister's efforts being described as having 'assumed heroic proportions'. Misgivings about the fate of Czechoslovakia were not prevalent. The *Financial Times* reflected the mood of the markets in declaring that 'dismemberment is a painful thing for a proud country to contemplate' but added that 'it possesses the one virtue that it will have spared countless million the horrors of a war more intense and destructive even than that of 1914–18'. How wrong can one be? At Lloyd's the *Lutine* Bell was struck in celebration and from both Lloyd's and the Stock Exchange Chamberlain's health was drunk and congratulatory telegrams despatched to Downing Street. The verdict of Sir Charles Addis, a banker with the Hong Kong and Shanghai Bank, echoed that of Edward VII at the end of the Boer war, 'Peace with honour. The Consols I bought two days ago at 66 are today quoted 75'.

Mustn't Embarrass a Lady

The exchange was better equipped to cope with the outbreak of war in 1939 than it had been in 1914, closing for only six days, and for one day in 1945 when the building was bombed. There were changes, however, some of which pointed to the future. In March 1942 two stockbroking firms each sought permission to employ a woman as a clerk. The two women would not be able to trade on the floor of the exchange but nevertheless a month passed before the committee voted by twelve votes to eleven to admit Mrs Miller and Mrs Judd to their posts. Their presence had one unforeseen consequence. A broker called Barton, who later claimed that he 'had a severe attack in the morning of kidney trouble owing to having stones, and took gin to relieve the pain' was consequently 'so drunk that he should not be allowed in the Stock Exchange' in the words of a witness. Barton was warned as to his conduct, not for being drunk but because he had sworn in the presence of a lady when greeting another broker with the words 'Here comes another f***ing Jew'. Racial abuse and drunkenness were less offensive than embarrassing a lady!

11

The Post-War Stock Exchange and the Big Bang

At the end of the war Britain's economy was in ruins, like many of its cities. The priority of the Labour government was to create the welfare state and rebuild British industry, sometimes nationalising it in the process. The needs of private investors were very low in the government's priorities, not helped by the attitudes of the chancellors, the ascetic Sir Stafford Cripps and the cerebral High Gaitskell. A shortage of foreign currency, accompanied by severe exchange controls that effectively prevented investors from moving their money out of the country, put most overseas investments out of reach so what funds were available tended to be invested in Britain. The City remained wedded to the idea that the pound sterling's status as a reserve currency would ensure that Britain remained at the top table of international finance, not far behind the United States, and so when sterling was devalued by 30 per cent in September 1949, it was a severe blow. Membership of the Stock Exchange became so unattractive that in May 1951 a 'nomination' was purchased from retiring members for as little as £10 and many remained unsold, retiring members failing to sell their nominations at any price in the early 1950s. In the circumstances it is not surprising that the annual ritual of re-election to membership at this time did not require a high standard of behaviour. Defaulting on a deal would lead to expulsion but short of that a member's behaviour had to be unusually offensive if he was to fail to be re-elected, as in the case of a broker called Cunningham whose re-election in 1946 was opposed on the grounds that:

He is continually collecting cigarette ends from the tins at the inside doors of the House [i.e. the exchange] rummaging the waste-paper baskets for newspapers or anything he may desire, picking up cigarette-ends at two local railway stations ... he is dirty, his clothes disgusting and he smells horribly.

Cunningham was nevertheless re-elected for another year though women and foreigners, of course, remained beyond the pale.

The Cult of the Equity

As the economy recovered in the 1950s under a more sympathetic Conservative administration, and with help from the Marshall Plan, which injected American money into the still ailing European economy, the so-called 'cult of the equity' benefited from two developments. First, more workers were paying into contributory pensions, obliging the managers of the pension funds to seek new outlets for their investments. This encouraged previously conservative fund managers to invest a larger proportion of their assets in shares rather than bonds and gilt-edged securities. In 1949 the stockbrokers Phillips and Drew were advising clients to invest 10 per cent in shares; by 1956 this had grown to 35 per cent. Yet it was still difficult to persuade bankers and fund managers to invest in innovative securities. In the 1950s the young Edward du Cann, later to become an MP and chairman of the Conservative party, searched the City for investors in a new unit trust management company, arguing that it would attract small investors. He received a very frosty reception but he persisted and launched Unicorn Unit Trust which enjoyed immediate success, attracted many imitators from those who had scorned it, and continues to flourish.

During the 1950s and early 1960s, at a time of low inflation and industrial expansion, the markets rose consistently and the exchange prospered. The camaraderie that characterised the Victorian exchange, which had been built in 1854 and survived until the 1970s, was caught in some later reminiscences by a stockbroker of the time who recalled the noise on the crowded exchange trading floor:

> I didn't think I could possibly stand it, because the noise and the people, as a Guards officer at Dunkirk so wittily said, appalled me. It was like being at a cocktail party without any drinks. But within a week I discovered the people were delightful and the noise I didn't even notice. It was like a rugger club, all boys together.

He went on to refer to such activities as throwing paper balls, soaking people's feet and habitually breaking into a chorus of 'Jerusalem' (for no reason anyone could remember) when an elderly dealer in gilts entered the room; while other pastimes involved setting fire to a newspaper which was being read by an inattentive dealer or snipping off the ties of the unwary. The crowded floor became less so when the Stock Exchange moved into a new multi-storey building in Throgmorton Street in 1972 but time was running out for the 'all boys together' habits of the 1970s exchange.

'A missionary on the shores of darkest Africa'

The jollity could not hide the fact that the insularity of the market was making it steadily less important in the world of global finance. Exchange controls (not removed until Mrs Thatcher came to office in 1979) continued to make it difficult to make significant investments overseas as had been the practice in the years before 1939. Stockbrokers remained partnerships, which encouraged caution in investment decisions and meant that their capital was limited. Foreign ownership of brokers and jobbers was for all practical purposes prohibited by the rules of the exchange itself. In the 1960s the Bank of England, under the governorship of Lord Cromer, himself one of the Baring family, had allowed foreign corporations to buy stakes in British financial institutions. Although when the American bank Continental Illinois declared that it was thinking of buying shares in a British merchant bank it was told by Sir Maurice Parsons, deputy governor of the bank, that while there was 'no formal barrier' it was a 'slightly delicate question'. In fact the Americans had already arrived and not everyone was at ease with them. In 1961 Jack Spall, with fourteen years' experience in one of the City's traditional British firms, joined the American brokers Merrill Lynch and was dumbfounded by the 'sudden display of wealth, which I was unused to'. He was particularly struck by the fact that, 'One of my colleagues was a woman, who was absolutely spot-on'. It would be twelve more years before women would be admitted to the floor of the Stock Exchange itself, and even then only after a great deal of reluctant deliberation. The first woman to be elected to membership, on 1 March 1973, was Mrs Muriel Wood, aged 66 who, as Miss Muriel Bailey, had first applied for membership seven years earlier, in 1966, after thirty-two years' service as a broker's clerk. Her earlier application had earned the response that, 'While there are no rules which specifically prohibit the admission of women members, any application from a woman candidate could involve matters of principle'. The 'matters of principle' were not specified but they presumably took seven years to resolve. As late as 1980 a young Harvard-educated American woman called Kimberley Albright felt that she was 'a missionary on the shores of darkest Africa' when making a presentation to a group of City grandees.

Fixed commissions and the rigid division between brokers and jobbers did not make for efficiency and were in effect anti-competitive. Those who worked in the exchange could earn a comfortable living without too much effort but London's position as a financial hub was being eroded. There was, moreover, a degree of complacency, reminiscent of the 'rugger club', which did not make for efficiency. When the future MP Jonathan Aitken sought Britain's thrusting entrepreneurs he was shocked by what he found in Capel Court. He found a fellow Etonian, in a family business, who arrived at the office at about 10.15 a.m. and left at 4 p.m. unless he'd been out the previous night in which case he would arrive later. Business was more likely to be conducted at deb (debutante) dances than in boardrooms. Insider dealing (making use of information not available to the market as a whole to gain an advantage) was frowned upon but not made illegal until 1980. Others thought that the most successful dealers were not the Etonians but barrow boys, raucous, ruthless and unapologetic who would otherwise be selling vegetables in Berwick Street and 'hot gear' in Bermondsey Market rather than shares. There were some hopeful signs. At Warburgs, known as The Night Club in the City, still dominated by the redoubtable Sigmund Warburg, desks were occupied by 9 a.m. and were still in use at 7 p.m. The fortunes of the exchange had recovered to the extent that, whereas 'nominations' had been virtually worthless in the early 1950s, by the late 1960s they were being bought for about £1,500. At the same time membership of the New York Stock Exchange was costing $200,000, a sad reflection of the extent to which the fortunes of the two institutions had diverged since London was the centre of world finance before 1914.

'In danger of becoming a backwater'

Following the abolition of exchange controls in October 1979, which the exchange naturally welcomed, it heard some alarming news. The Office of Fair Trading (OFT) announced that it was going to take action against what it regarded as the anti-competitive practices of the exchange, such as fixed commissions and the difficulties that foreign institutions encountered in entering the market. The exchange received some support in its distress from a surprising quarter. Harold Wilson, the former Labour Prime Minister, had chaired a committee on the City and he wrote to Margaret Thatcher arguing that the OFT case should be dropped. The Prime Minister, however, who had her own serious reservations about the way the City managed its affairs, was implacable and saw no reason why the exchange should be exempted from rules which applied to other businesses. In 1983, after the Conservatives' resounding general election victory, the chairman of the Stock Exchange Council, Sir Nicholas Goodison, opened negotiations with Cecil Parkinson, the new Trade Secretary. Parkinson consulted the new Chancellor, Nigel Lawson who, as a former financial journalist, had a good working knowledge of the City. Lawson suggested that the City was suffering from woeful undercapitalisation and that, 'while the City of London remained one of the world leaders, if not the world leader, across a whole range of financial markets, such as the foreign exchange market, in the securities market it was in danger of becoming a backwater'. By the time of the negotiations the London Stock Exchange, once the undisputed world leader, accounted for one thirteenth of the turnover of New York and one fifth that of Tokyo.

The deal that Parkinson concluded, with advice from the Chancellor, contained five elements. The minimum commission system would be abolished; the prohibition on brokers also acting as jobbers would be removed, the latter becoming known as 'market makers'; an appeal tribunal would 'reveal and if appropriate over-rule the Council's decision to refuse an application for Membership'; the appeals committee would have a majority who were not Stock Exchange members of the Council; and in liaison with the Bank of England lay members would be brought on to the Council. The closed shop was now opening and the way was clear for the Big Bang.

The Big Bang and the Future: 'Grotesquely overpaid jobs'

In 2010 the Cambridge philosopher Simon Blackburn drew attention to a recent phenomenon in the life of the City that helped to explain the financial meltdown that had begun with the collapse of Northern Rock and continued with the demise of Lehman brothers and the Libor scandal:

> It is well known that a large part of the financial meltdown of the last couple of years is because young whizz-kids from mathematics and physics are flocking into grotesquely overpaid jobs in the City and there, having no smidgeon of an education in humanistic fields, making fantastical models and predictions in complete disregard of the real world.

Many would argue that the financial problems which afflicted the City, and the world, from 2008, had their origins in the cultural changes that led up to the Big Bang of 27 October 1986 and which restored the City's position as one of the world's leading financial markets but also contained destructive seeds.

The Banks Invade the Exchange

In October 1983, as the City began to confront the future which had been mapped out in the agreement between Parkinson and Goodison, Jacob Rothschild warned of a 'nightmarishly complicated scenario' dominated by 'the worldwide financial service company and the international commercial bank with a global trading competence'. He warned his audience of City grandees that the American investment bank Salomons had generated more profit in 1982 ($500 million) than had all the firms trading on the London Stock Exchange put together. For the moment, outside firms such as banks, British or foreign, could purchase a maximum of 29.9 per cent of a member firm of the exchange though few believed that this restriction would last very long. On 4 November, shortly after Jacob Rothschild's speech, America's largest bank, Citicorp, bought a 29.9 per cent stake in the brokers Vickers da Costa. Other similar deals followed in quick succession. By the end of 1984, according to one informed estimate, over a billion pounds had been spent buying thirty-six stock exchange firms, to the great profit of the partners in the firms concerned, until very few independent brokers were left, Cazenove being the exception amongst the larger houses. At the same time there was an expensive scramble to recruit experienced jobbers from the small number (about a dozen) of large jobbing partnerships to create the new species of 'market maker' within the 'worldwide financial service companies' of Rothschild's doom-laden prediction. One consequence of the purchase of partnerships by large banks was that the former partners, by becoming shareholders in their new owners, could afford to be less cautious in their investments and risk-taking. A partner who made a foolish investment could find his personal fortune at stake, whereas a shareholder, who benefited from limited liability, stood to lose his shares but little else. From now on, risk did not carry the danger of personal ruin and many believe this explained the frantic and in some cases disastrous risk-taking which characterised the first decade of the twentieth century.

The First Privatisation

Other coincidental developments at this time were themselves significant for the future of the City. In February 1984 the Stock Exchange Council voted to end the minimum commission system (after Big Bang commissions disappeared altogether on many large transactions) and in the same month the *Financial Times* launched its Footsie index of a hundred leading shares, a clearer indication of the state of the stock market (and often of the economy) than any previous measure. In November 1984 the first steps in the Thatcher government's privatisation of state-owned assets saw the public offering of almost £4 billion of shares in British Telecom, the largest issue of shares the City had ever seen. The process by which the shares came to market reflected no credit on the City itself, rather reflecting its still cautious and conservative culture. The Prime Minister, never a great admirer of the City and its ways, was determined to press ahead and the task of selling the shares was awarded to the merchant bank Kleinwort Benson, headed by Sir

Martin Jacomb. But when the Chancellor, Nigel Lawson, attended a meeting of City grandees he remarked that, with the exception of Jacomb, 'each and every one of them roundly declared that the privatisation was impossible: the capital market simply was not large enough to absorb it'. In fact the issue was over-subscribed five times over, the shares approached 100 per cent premium and frantic scenes followed when dealings began on the floor of the Stock Exchange. The City embraced future privatisations with greater enthusiasm, notably that of British Gas with its 'Tell Sid' campaign but again failed to cover itself in glory with the sale of BP shares. In October 1987 the biggest privatisation to date, of over £7 billion of British Petroleum shares, was fully underwritten at £3.30 but when the market crashed on 20 October and the shares fell in value the government was urged by the underwriters to cancel the issue, a view that received some support from the Bank of England. Nigel Lawson, with strong support from Margaret Thatcher who was 'outraged' by the City's behaviour, declared in parliament that he 'was surprised' by the underwriters' reaction, dismissed their requests and offered them a much less attractive deal: an offer they couldn't refuse.

The Bank of England. (Wikimedia Commons, Adrian Pingstone)

New Technology

In the preparations for the Big Bang, firms were investing large sums in computer technology that would enable them to trade shares by telephone or online, without the need for the face to face trading that had been customary since the time of Garraway's and Jonathan's. To accommodate the new technology, huge dealing rooms with banks of computers replaced the intimate offices associated with the traditional broking businesses and this in turn generated the need for more modern office space in the City, creating a boom in the construction industry as old buildings were demolished or converted to create the necessary space. The atrium came into fashion as an appendage to spacious, open-plan dealing rooms with banks of computers manned by men (and a growing number of women) who spent their days shouting into telephones or bellowing at one another across the intervening floor space. One of the first consents to a conversion given by the City Corporation was for the old Billingsgate fish market though, as we have seen, this would find other uses. Much more ambitious schemes followed, beginning with the Broadgate development near Liverpool Street Station but the greatest of all resulted from a visit by Dr Michael von Clemm, the American chairman of Credit Suisse First Boston's London operation, to a neglected area of London in search of premises for a packaging plant for a chain of upmarket restaurants. His search took him to the Isle of Dogs, long discarded as part of the London docks, and to a disused banana warehouse there. His bank had long been searching vainly for suitable premises within the City itself but the possibilities presented by Docklands as an alternative to the Square Mile were clearer to Dr von Clemm than they had been to others. Michael Cassidy, chairman of the City Corporation's Planning Committee, took up the idea and a derelict wasteland was transformed into a new financial hub. The Canary Wharf scheme, linked to the centre by the extended Jubilee Line and the Docklands Light Railway, would eventually accommodate Europe's three tallest towers and over 9 million square feet of office space.

A Bigger Bang than Anticipated

On 27 October 1986, the day usually described as Big Bang, the long-heralded switch to computerised trading took place. The trading systems stood up reasonably well to the increased volumes of business though the back offices, still often dealing in paper systems, struggled to complete deals in a timely manner. The leisurely days of 10 a.m. starts and 4 p.m. finishes that had surprised Jonathan Aitken were gone forever and for more reasons than unfinished paperwork. An 8 a.m. start was essential to catch the Tokyo Exchange before it closed while New York opened at 3 p.m. London time. Now that

Paternoster Square, St Paul's, the new home of the Stock Exchange, which is to the right of the picture. (Wikimedia Commons, gren)

dealing required no face-to-face meeting, traders at their computers could use contacts in both time zones to generate profits. At the same time, in the absence of exchange controls, London began to deal in European markets much as it had done before 1914, and before the launch of the Euro currency in 2002 it was handling far more transactions in Deutschmarks than Frankfurt was. Other consequences followed. By January 1987 the Stock Exchange's trading floor was deserted as traders took to their computers and in the words of one trader, 'We've got a viewing gallery with nothing to see'. In 2004 the exchange, which had become an administrative and regulatory body rather than a trading centre, moved from its multi-storey building on Throgmorton Street to smaller premises in Paternoster Square, close to St Paul's Cathedral. It is no longer possible to visit the Stock Exchange, as there is nothing of interest to see. There have been a number of attempts by outside bodies to merge with or take over the London Stock Exchange, most notably in 2011 by NASDAQ (the National Association of Securities Dealers Automated Quotations) an exchange based in New York. All have so far failed. New computerised trading systems were introduced and, after some early setbacks, settled down to provide the service the market needed though not without setbacks. On 5 April 2000, the last day of the tax year, the computer systems crashed, an event described by one newspaper as, 'The day London's Stock Exchange died'. Reports of its death were greatly exaggerated and trading resumed in the afternoon but a veteran trader, Brian Winterflood, summed up the feelings of many, 'This is the IT world for you. You drop your calculator and the battery falls out and suddenly you haven't got a brain'.

Bad Practices

Shortly after Big Bang took effect, investigations began into malpractice; the enquiry process helped by the ability to track computerised share dealings and even telephone calls. In November 1986 Geoffrey Collier, a trader at the bank Morgan Grenfell, resigned and was subsequently given a suspended prison sentence for insider dealing while managers at the same bank were found to have helped Guinness to take over the Distillers Company, in the face of a rival bid, by manipulating the value of Guinness's shares. Wealthy individuals had been encouraged to purchase large numbers of Guinness shares on the understanding that if they fell in value they would be reimbursed by the company itself once the takeover had been completed: echoes of the South Sea Bubble. Prison sentences followed and Morgan Grenfell, one of the most respected merchant banks in the City, was bought in 1990 by a German bank and the name was dropped. It was not the City's finest hour.

'Loadsamoney'

A further consequence of the more frenetic (some would say more enterprising) dealing culture was the inflation of salaries. Shortly before the Big Bang it was reported that Morgan Grenfell had recruited a four-man team from the stockbrokers Grieveson Grant for a remuneration package exceeding £1 million. This was a sign of things to come, a process that did not impress Margaret Thatcher: 'on salaries in the City I am the first to say this does cause me great concern. I understand the resentment'. It prompted the comic Harry Enfield to introduce the world to the obnoxious, wallet-flapping Cockney plasterer 'Loadsamoney' who spawned his own hit song and live tour. Some thought that the barrow boys and Old Etonians of the 1960s were being replaced by workaholic geeks with skills in computer science and the construction of complex mathematic algorithms which, by analysing past events, would forecast future trends and lead their fortunate owners inexorably to pots of gold at the end of every rainbow. The pressure to perform produced some worrying outcomes and some tragic ones. A drinking culture, which had long been evident in the City, became pervasive, with the last train from Liverpool Street to Essex on Fridays becoming known as the Vomit Comet while a descendant of the most eminent City dynasty of all, Amschel Rothschild, hanged himself in a Paris hotel in July 1996. Those who knew him believed that he would never have gone into the City but for family pressure and that he was quite unsuited to the post-1986 City.

Giving Away the Keys

At the same time there was increasing anxiety in some quarters about the degree to which ownership of City institutions had fallen into foreign hands, notably American, German and Japanese banks. In October 1997 the *Daily Telegraph* announced 'the demise of the City of London' because so many institutions had fallen into foreign ownership. Three years later *The Independent* suggested that this process had 'given the keys to the City of London to its global competitors' who could, if they wished, 'set about dismantling it'. This did not prevent the market continuing to rise on the back of the dotcom boom, the FTSE Index reaching just short of 7,000 as the millennium approached. Sixteen years later the market struggles to hover around 6,500 but there is no sign of the City losing its position in world financial markets. The critical mass of traders in London, the availability of office space in the City and Docklands, the skills in dealing that the City has developed over centuries and, not least, the English language in which so much of the world's commerce is transacted have all conspired to maintain London's place at the centre of the world's securities business, alongside or, in places ahead of, New York and Tokyo. The recent troubles of the Eurozone and its evident long-term problems have tended to confirm the view of the former governor of the Bank of England, Eddie George, that 'The Euro is just a bigger Deutschmark. We have seemed to do perfectly satisfactorily handling the mark, just as we have the dollar and yen. I am sure that the City will cope'. He could have added that London had long been, and remained, by far the largest market in the trading of bonds denominated in dollars.

The City's coping mechanisms, however, failed to foresee the collapse of market confidence which began with the failure of Northern Rock in 2007 and was soon reflected in other markets, notably Spain and the USA, where unwise loans made against the security of property of doubtful value led to the failures of property owners and banks. The problems were compounded by the trading in derivatives, supposedly based on real assets but often based on thin air. Many American subprime loans were based on the assumption that a loan to one person with a poor credit history and low income was unwise, but that if a trader 'packaged' such a loan with many other similar ones then somehow all would be well. And if he could sell the 'packages' to other people (many were bought by German banks who needed investments for their mounting pile of Euros earned by Germany's exporters) then that was even better. When the queen, on a visit to the London School of Economics, asked why no one had seen the disaster coming, no one could answer her. Explanations abounded after the event but the wisdom of hindsight is no use when it's needed. To be fair, many did anticipate the troubles of the Euro whose notes and coins replaced many national currencies in January 2002. Nigel Lawson, John Major and Gordon Brown all had misgivings about the viability of a currency serving such a diverse range of economies as Germany, Greece, the Netherlands and Portugal and it is to their credit that Britain stood back from joining the Eurozone.

Derivatives

Derivatives are securities based upon the performance or behaviour of something that is not directly owned by the holder of the derivative. For example no one owns the weather though it may be crucial to the harvest of coffee, cocoa or other commodities whose availability and price have a direct effect upon a manufacturer of chocolate or drinks. Farmers and theme parks are similarly affected. So these groups may enter into a contract whereby the owner of the farm or theme park agrees to pay a certain sum in return for a guaranteed payout if rain falls at certain times. It is a means of 'hedging', or insuring, against adverse weather. Similar arrangements can be made to guard against rises or falls in commodity prices or share indexes. Derivative contracts can themselves be traded, being sold by one trader to another and they can fulfil a useful purpose in stabilising volatile markets provided that those trading them understand what they are and act within reasonable limits. Problems arise when the traders of derivative contracts don't fully understand what they represent or risk sums that they can't afford. Huge sums can be at stake for small outlays as Nick Leeson and Barings discovered when Leeson placed a bet on a rise in the Japanese stock market, which collapsed when the Kobe earthquake struck. Many of the contracts traded on LIFFE (see page 102) are derivatives.

In 2014 London lists almost 3,000 companies from sixty countries. Of the total, about 1,200 are listed on the Alternative Investment Market (AIM) which was launched by the exchange in 1995 to replace the more informal Unlisted Securities Market and accommodates the flotation of smaller companies not yet ready for a full listing. London is the second largest centre for trading securities after New York, with companies on the London Stock Exchange valued at $3.5 trillion compared with the New York Exchange's $16.3 trillion, $3.2 trillion in Tokyo and $1.3 trillion for Frankfurt. London has proved popular for the listing of corporations based in Russia and other relatively new markets and has more funds listed from emerging markets than any other exchange, with 158 against New York's 126. London also accounts for 36 per cent of all transactions in foreign exchange, substantially more than any other centre and it is for this reason that the London market price of currencies is used by international bodies such as the International Monetary Fund for their own purposes.

So was Simon Blackburn right in suggesting that 'whizz kids in mathematics and physics' were driving the City and the economy to the abyss over which Northern Rock, Lehman brothers, Greece, Portugal, Ireland, Spain and others have fallen? Was it all the fault of the traders in the financial markets, bent only on short-term bonuses regardless of the broader effects? Or do the rest of us bear some responsibility? Perhaps it was the fault of politicians for choosing 'light touch' regulatory regimes designed to attract investors. Conversely was it the fault of financial regulators for averting their gazes from the fact that assets were becoming over-valued and lending too generous? Or was it our own fault as consumers for borrowing more money than we could afford to repay?

12

The London International Financial Futures and Options Exchange (LIFFE)

Greek Philosophers and Option Traders

One does not expect to find a link between the philosophers of ancient Greece and young men in striped jackets shouting into mobile phones in the City of London. Yet the first record of options trading is to be found in the work of the Greek philosopher Aristotle. In his work *Politics* he tells the story of Thales, a philosopher of the sixth century BC from the Greek city of Miletus, now on the Turkish coast of the Aegean. Thales, of whom Aristotle wrote that he had designed 'a financial device which contains a principle of universal application', was presumably a student of the weather since he anticipated an exceptional olive harvest for the forthcoming autumn. He therefore entered into contracts with owners of olive presses for the option of exclusive use of their equipment once the olives were harvested, paying them a small deposit in return for such use at an agreed price. The price he negotiated was advantageous to Thales because the press owners, who knew nothing of the likely harvest, wanted a guarantee that their presses would be used and therefore agreed to a relatively low price, a form of 'hedging' against a poor harvest. Once the harvest was in, and as bountiful as Thales had predicted, Thales was able to sell his right to use the presses to the olive farmers at a high price because demand for the presses exceeded capacity. Thales thereby made a substantial profit but the important point is that at no point in the process did Thales either own any olives or use the presses. This is a characteristic of trading in options, or futures, the right to do or own something in the future, a right which the trader may exercise himself or, more often, choose to sell to someone else.

'Calls' and 'Puts'; Options and Futures

The trading of futures contracts began on the London Stock Exchange in the early nineteenth century. These were simply the right to buy (or sell) a security or commodity on a future date at a given price. So a brewer, for example, who wanted to be sure that he could purchase hops or barley at a given price, regardless of the fortunes of the harvest, would enter into a contract to buy at an agreed price and would pay a fee for the service to a dealer. A farmer who wanted to be sure of the price he would receive for his crop would enter into a similar agreement to sell. The right to buy was known as a 'call' option and the right to sell as a 'put' option. But if a trader, having taken out a contract to buy or sell, was unable to sell on that contract to another trader then he was obliged to honour the contract which might involve selling at a price lower than the market conditions warranted or buying at a higher price than he would otherwise need to pay. Thales, if he had misjudged the harvest and couldn't sell the options to olive growers, would have lost his deposit but wouldn't have had to pay to use the presses. But if Cadbury's entered into a futures contract to buy cocoa at a high price and the price then fell they'd still have to buy the cocoa at the high price agreed and put it down to experience unless they could sell the contract to someone else in the meantime.

Such contracts are thus risky for those entering into them and by 1821 the number of dealers defaulting on such contracts as these (and having to quit the exchange) had reached a level where there was a proposal to ban them altogether. As a compromise a fourteen-day limit was placed on such deals (thereby rendering many of them unworkable) but the practice survived despite the prohibition and remains a feature of the market to this day, albeit without such time limits.

The Windy City

The first modern futures exchange operating on a large scale was established in Chicago, the 'windy city' (so called because of the talkative nature of the residents or the breeze from Lake Michigan, according to whom you believe). Situated at a strategic point on the Great Lakes it was a natural centre for the collection, distribution and trading of livestock and grain and the first futures contract, on corn, was written on 13 March 1851 under the auspices of the Chicago Board of Trade. By 1875 purchases of grain in Chicago amounted to $200 million a year but futures contracts, speculating on the prices at which the grain would eventually be delivered, were ten times that level. The Chicago Board of Trade had become primarily a market in the price of grain rather than in the product itself. Chicago remains one of the world's leading centres for the trading of agricultural produce. Where Chicago led London soon followed. On 1 May 1888 the London Produce Clearing House (later called the International Commodities Clearing House or ICCH) began to trade in future contracts in sugar and coffee, transactions in 2.26 million bags of coffee and 1.27 million bags of sugar being cleared in its first year.

Financial Turbulence

In 1944, at Bretton Woods in New Hampshire, the leading Western nations had set up a monetary framework that was designed to replace the unstable currency systems that had helped to make the depression of the 1930s worse. The new system was underpinned by the US dollar, which could be converted to gold at a price of $35 an ounce. Other countries were obliged to maintain their economies in such a way that their currencies fluctuated in relation to the dollar only within very narrow bands, thus enabling international transactions to be conducted in the knowledge that the currencies in which contracts were made would not collapse in value. In 1971, following a period of economic turbulence caused in part by American expenditure on the war in Vietnam, the value of the United States dollar came under pressure and was decoupled from the price of gold, thereby plunging the world's currencies into an uncertain state of affairs. Two years later, in 1973, the Organisation of Petroleum Exporting Countries (OPEC) increased the price of oil dramatically, causing further disruptions to world markets. Exchange rates began to fluctuate amongst the world's major currencies to a degree that would have been unprecedented a decade earlier, introducing an additional element of uncertainty into the world of commodity trading. A company dependent upon corn, cocoa, beef, oil or other raw materials now had to take into account not only the fluctuating future cost of the commodity itself but also the fact that the currency in which the commodity was bought and sold could change in value. Since most companies, especially in industries like food, oil and plastics, have a substantial proportion of their costs in such commodities, this additional risk could have a ruinous influence upon their profits. In 1971, the year the dollar abandoned the gold standard, therefore, Chicago created the International Monetary Market to offer futures contracts in major currencies including the dollar, the pound and the Deutschmark.

'Money is a raw material'

The problems of turbulence in commodity prices (notably oil) and in currency values were not confined to the USA. In Britain the 1970s were marked by high inflation, high (and hence inflationary) wage settlements, rising unemployment, high interest rates, declining competitiveness and a pound falling in value against other currencies. In 1978 an article in the *Investor's Chronicle* drew attention to the fact that, 'Money is a raw material of business, but a material at whose cost British business can now only guess.' The author of the article, Christopher Fildes, reported that London traders had been visiting Chicago to learn how that market had created a mechanism for 'hedging' against changes in currency values, only to discover that colleagues from the International Commodities Clearing House (ICCH) were already working on the idea. The object of the new market at this stage was not to create profit-making opportunities in their own right but to create certainty for corporate treasurers who were having to make educated guesses about the future value of currencies in which they would have to make or receive payments. Some companies sought to avoid the problems of high interest by borrowing in stronger foreign currencies. Disaster followed when loans in Deutschmarks had to be repaid from profits in declining pounds and this caused serious problems for companies like Lyons who adopted this strategy.

The impetus for change grew when, in 1979, Margaret Thatcher's government abolished exchange controls, removing barriers to the movement of sterling overseas which created a position similar to that which had existed prior to 1914 when the City had stood at the centre of the world's trade in products, services and capital. But whereas in 1914 the strong pound had been overwhelmingly the world's preferred currency with which to settle international payments, backed by Britain's industrial strength and the huge gold and currency reserves of the Bank of England, it was now much weaker in relation to currencies like the dollar, the yen, the Deutschmark and the Swiss Franc. With the value of the pound fluctuating from day to day, sometimes alarmingly in relation to the latest balance of payments figures or news of another strike, banks and companies were at the mercy of forces beyond their control.

LIFFE to the rescue

On 30 September 1982 the governor of the Bank of England, Gordon Richardson, entered the Royal Exchange and rang a bell to begin the first day's trading on London's new markets in futures and options. The bell was a relic of the Victorian exchange, rebuilt after the fire of 1838, and had been found by an engineer who was working to put the exchange into a condition fit for its new use. Since 1979 the Royal Exchange had been closed to the public because of its poor state, its few moments of glory falling shortly before Christmas each year when charities were allowed to use it to sell Christmas cards. It now gained a new lease of life as the home of the London International Financial Futures and Options Exchange (LIFFE), a new market that had been in preparation for two and a half years. It would soon merge with other exchanges so that it traded futures and options in currencies, shares, agricultural commodities, bonds (including those issued by foreign governments), interest rates (in effect bets on whether interest rates would rise or fall) and even the movement of stock markets. It enabled corporations, including banks, to 'cover' themselves against fluctuations in prices and rates that could be critical for their businesses. It did not remove uncertainty but enabled businesses to manage it and guard against its worst consequences in a volatile world.

Open to All, Including Tic Tac Men

Applications for membership of the new exchange were invited from any who could pay the initial membership fee of £20,000 (later increased) and show that they had adequate resources and expertise. When the exchange opened the biggest single category of membership was foreign banks (56) followed by commodity brokers (53) and UK banks (32) though they also included some individuals. The initial means of trading was by 'open outcry'. Traders, clad in colourful striped jackets to denote the company for which they worked, operated in the trading 'pits', each pit accommodating a separate financial product. The traders would call out offers for contracts in accordance with instructions from their colleagues in booths outside the pits. Such was the noise that communications between traders and booths was usually done by hand movements reminiscent of those used by bookies' tic tac men at racecourses. Hand signals would indicate 'sell' or 'buy' according to whether the palm of the hand was outwards from the body or inwards towards it; and quantities would be indicated by touching various parts of the face. The Royal Exchange had never been noisier. Moreover the new exchange's rules included elements that would later be copied by its older brother the Stock Exchange. From the first day, foreign institutions were welcomed to membership, there were no minimum commissions and traders could be both principals and agents (jobbers and brokers) arrangements that were still being resisted by the Stock Exchange.

£Billions

The market soon developed a life of its own, with traders making money by trading the contracts amongst themselves on small margins but in huge volumes. In the early days trading levels were modest but they swiftly rose so that within a few years a turnover of hundreds of billions of pounds per day was being recorded. On 16 September 1992, Black Wednesday, when the pound was forced out of the European Exchange Rate Mechanism, the traders in the striped blazers in the LIFFE pits were shouting themselves hoarse all day and many of them made fortunes from the pound's misfortunes as the exchange turned over £254 billion. Since 2007 LIFFE has been part of a network of exchanges trading under its own name as part of NYSE (New York Stock Exchange) Euronext and remains the dominant force in its market.

As business grew the Royal Exchange trading floor became too small. It was briefly suggested that it should now move to the Stock Exchange building whose trading floor had become empty since the Big Bang of 1986. On 13 December 1991 the exchange bell was rung for the last time and the following Monday trading resumed at new premises at Cannon Bridge House, opposite Cannon Street Station, with a trading floor of 25,000sq.ft, two and a half times that of the Royal Exchange. However, screen trading, as with the Stock Exchange, had begun in 1998 and a proposal for a further move to even

LIFFE trader, mobile phone to ear, near Cannon Street station. (Statue by Stephen Melton, Wikimedia Commons, QuentinUK)

larger premises at a refurbished Spitalfields market was abandoned when, in November 2000 the last of the open outcry pits was closed, the garish jackets discarded and the exchange followed the Stock Exchange in a move to purely electronic screen trading. The statue of a LIFFE trader, mobile phone to his ear, stands opposite Cannon Street Station as a reminder of how things once were.

13

The London Metal Exchange: The Last 'Open Outcry'

Trading by 'open outcry' survives in the London Metal Exchange, now based at No. 56, Leadenhall Street. The trading of metals was one of many markets that originated in the Royal Exchange in the reign of Elizabeth I and later in the surrounding coffee houses, particularly the Jerusalem coffee house off Cornhill. A merchant with a cargo of metal to sell would draw a chalk ring on the floor and call out 'Change' which was an invitation to those who wished to buy to assemble around the circle and make their bids. Until the advent of the Industrial Revolution the United Kingdom was self-sufficient in metals like copper and tin but by the nineteenth century supplies of such metals from Cornwall and elsewhere were no longer sufficient for the economy's growing needs and imports became essential. The present market, the London

Above: Lloyd's of London. (Lloyd's website)

Left: The London Metal Exchange, 56 Leadenhall Street, London's last 'open outcry' market. (Wikimedia Commons, Kreepin Deth)

Metal Market and Exchange Company was founded in 1877 above a hat shop in Lombard Court for the trading of copper which took about three months to reach London from Chile, its main source until copper was later discovered in Zambia. Tin was brought from Malaya, a journey that had been shortened to three months by the opening of the Suez Canal in 1869. For this reason it was customary for a price to be agreed for delivery after three months, a practice which, for some contracts, persists in the market to this day. Lead and zinc were soon added to the metals traded followed by aluminium, nickel, steel and other metals and, for a short time, plastics. Precious metals, gold and silver, are not traded on the exchange. Each year the exchange accounts for over 100 million trades and 12 trillion dollars.

Ring-dealing members of the exchange, of which there are at present twelve member companies, are entitled to trade in the ring, a small circular space on the trading floor reminiscent of the original chalk circle in the Jerusalem coffee house, in which one metal at a time is traded for two sessions of five minutes each day. As the time for trading the metal arrives, the appropriate symbol is displayed in the ring (symbols originating with thirteenth-century alchemists) and those members who wish to trade gather in the ring and call out the prices they are prepared to pay. The official settlement price, on which contracts are agreed, is the last price offered before the bell sounds at the end of the five-minute period. Besides recording a daily settlement price the market offers opportunities both to trade the metals and to take out hedges against rises or falls in their prices. It has not always been a harmonious place in which to do business. In 1976 Geraldine Bridgewater became the first female trader to be admitted to the floor of the exchange and was greeted by hisses, boos and cries of 'Get out! Get out! No women allowed'. One trader even aimed a kick at her shins. Not the exchange's finest hour! She later wrote an account of her experiences as a ring trader in *Ring of Truth* (2007).

WHEN CAN I VISIT?

The exchange has a viewing gallery which is open to visitors from 12 p.m. to 1.30 p.m. and from 3.30 p.m. to 4.15 p.m. Monday to Friday. The website facilitieshelpdesk@lme.com allows you to book a visit in advance.

14

Lloyd's of London: Spreading the Risks to Shipping and to a Moustache

The concept of shipping insurance was first enshrined in an Act of Parliament in 1601 which, having outlined the perils of 'any great adventure, specially into remote parts' explained that by spreading the risks of such ventures amongst many, any loss 'lighteth rather easily upon many, rather than heavily upon few'. Insurance policies underwritten by individuals of means were sufficiently common by the mid-seventeenth century for them to be found in the diary of Samuel Pepys. On 23 November 1663 Pepys's *Diary* records that he had been sorely tempted to subscribe to a policy on a ship which was overdue but which he, as an Admiralty clerk, knew to be safe in port. Instead, as he recorded, 'I went like an ass to Alderman Bakewell and told him of it'. This, to his regret, cost him £100 though if he had succumbed to temptation he would have been guilty of what, three centuries later, became known as 'insider dealing'. Besides, within a few days Pepys had made £320 from a bribe on insuring some Admiralty cargoes. The marine insurance business also benefited from London's pre-eminence as a port, a contemporary writing that, 'It may be said without vanity that no River in the World can show a braver sight of Ships than are commonly to be seen like a floating forest from Blackwall to London Bridge'.

A Coffee House

Edward Lloyd opened his coffee house in Tower Street in about 1688. Tower Street was the name then given to a ward of the City of London, in the vicinity of the Tower of London and close to that part of the river known as the Pool of London, the heart of London's port. Little is known of Edward Lloyd beyond the fact that he was a member of the Framework Knitter's Company, a livery company formed a few years earlier, having been incorporated by

Oliver Cromwell in 1657. The first evidence of his coffee house is found in an advertisement in the *London Gazette* in 1688 offering, 'A reward of a guinea for information about stolen watches, claimable from Mr Edward Lloyd's Coffee House in Tower Street', an advertisement which sounds suspiciously like those placed a few years later by the 'thief taker' (and thief) Jonathan Wilde (see page 60). The coffee house was much frequented by sailors, merchants and shipowners and Edward Lloyd, like his contemporaries at Jonathan's and Garraway's (see pages 55 et seq.), provided his clientele with information about matters of interest to them such as the arrivals and departures of vessels and cargoes, losses at sea and prices. Conversation inevitably turned to shipping matters and specifically to insurance and it was perhaps for this reason that, at the end of 1691, Lloyd relocated his coffee shop to Lombard Street, close to the heart of London's banking and broking community.

Lombard Street became the heart of London's banking community in the Middle Ages because of the ingenuity of the bankers from Lombardy, in the vicinity of Milan in Italy. They had found a way of circumventing the mediaeval laws against usury, or lending money for interest payments. Jews of course were not affected by the laws but they were expelled from England by Edward I (who owed them money) in 1290. The Lombards stepped into the breach. The Lombards would accept an object of value such as gold or jewellery, advance money which was less than the value of the object and then return it when the owner paid them more than he had borrowed: a form of pawnbroking which amounted to banking by another name. After the Reformation of the sixteenth century the usury laws no longer applied but Lombard Street remained a centre of London's banking community, as it still does.

Insuring the Middle Passage

The new site for the coffee house in Lombard Street was also close to the General Post Office, established by Charles II in 1660, which was the principal source of shipping intelligence and it was in Lombard Street that Lloyd's first became the major centre for shipping insurance. A blue plaque in Lombard Street marks its former site, now the home of a bank. In 1696 Lloyd's began to publish *Lloyd's News*, a single sheet containing information about shipping matters for 'All gentlemen, Merchants or others' and costing one old penny. This was the predecessor of *Lloyd's List of shipping intelligence*, which began publication in 1734 as the definitive source of information about shipping matters. Edward Lloyd himself died in February 1713, this being announced in the *Flying Post* as, 'Died Mr Lloyd the Coffee-man in Lombard Street'. During these early years much of the insurance that was negotiated at Lloyd's was for slave ships in which British merchants held a dominant position. The trade was both profitable and hazardous, not least for the slaves. It is estimated that over 3 million people were carried into slavery by British ships before the trade was abolished in 1807, of which more than 10 per cent died on the notorious middle passage across the Atlantic, with over 1,000 ships lost. A shipowner seeking insurance would entrust a broker with the task of taking a policy to an appropriate number of wealthy individuals, each of whom would underwrite, or in effect guarantee, a proportion of the risk. The skill of the broker lay in recognising the creditworthiness and trustworthiness of the underwriters.

Unsavoury Practices Excluded

The years at Lombard Street attracted some disagreeable characters who found in insurance an outlet for exotic forms of gambling, the most unsavoury being a form of life insurance in which bets were placed on the life expectancy of someone who was known to be ill. In the words of a contemporary, when the unfortunate objects of such attention read in a newspaper 'that their lives had been insured at 90 per cent they despaired of all hopes; and thus their dissolution was hastened'. In 1769 some more respectable members of the Lloyd's Coffee House community set up New Lloyd's Coffee House nearby in Pope's Head Alley, close to the Royal Exchange, but as the business grew they soon sought more commodious accommodation. Seventy-nine underwriters and brokers each subscribed £100 towards new premises and in 1774 Lloyd's moved into the Royal Exchange itself. Although it continued to be referred to for some years as 'Lloyd's Coffee House' it had left behind the coffee house world and, while remaining a loose association of members, it had become a recognisable business, run by a committee and with a formal membership who each paid a fee to join. It was not incorporated until an Act of Parliament in 1871, the effect of the Act being to make it illegal for anyone who was not a recognised underwriting member at Lloyd's to put his name to a Lloyd's policy. Lloyd's had begun its long journey from an informal club of coffee house habitués to a well-regulated corporate body. The journey was to be marked by episodes of incompetence and dishonesty as well as some more glorious chapters.

John Julius Angerstein

Some of the names of the early underwriters have survived into the twenty-first century. John Robinson, trading then in Birchin Lane, off Cornhill, was the precursor of the travel agent and insurance broker Hogg Robinson, now listed on the Stock Exchange. One of the most dominant figures at Lloyd's at this time was John Julius Angerstein (1732–1823). Born in St Petersburg, of uncertain parentage but possibly the son of Empress Anna of Russia and a London businessman who traded in Russia, Andrew Thompson, John Angerstein settled in London in 1749 and worked in Thompson's London office before becoming one of the early underwriters at Lloyd's Coffee House. He was a shrewd investor and became so strongly associated with certain types of insurance that they became known as 'Julians' and it was claimed at the time that, 'When his name appeared on a policy it was a sufficient recommendation for the rest to follow where he led without further examination'. Acting as a broker he placed what was, and was to remain for more than a century, the largest ever insurance of a cargo of gold and other valuables to be brought from Vera Cruz in South America to London in a frigate called *Diana*, the insured value being £656,800. He promoted an Act of Parliament that forbade the owners of unseaworthy ships from changing their names in order to make them insurable. He also promoted a prize of £2,000, sponsored by Lloyd's, for the design of a lifeboat and devised an early state lottery which was adopted by Parliament as a tax-raising measure. He owned estates in Grenada in the West Indies that were worked by slaves and he benefited from Lloyd's underwriting of slave shipments but he also supported the Committee for the Relief of the Black Poor which had strong connections with abolitionists. In 1790, following a series of supposed attacks by the 'London Monster', who allegedly attacked ladies by sticking sharp objects in their bottoms, Angerstein offered a reward of £100 for his capture. This led to the arrest of an almost certainly innocent maker of artificial flowers called Rhynwick Williams who spent a few reasonably comfortable years in Newgate before being released and passing from history. Angerstein's handsome collection of paintings, which included works by Titian, Rubens, Rembrandt, Velazquez and some early drawings by Turner, formed the nucleus of the National Gallery which, before the construction of its present home in Trafalgar Square, were displayed in Angerstein's home in Pall Mall. A Lloyd's syndicate still bears his name, as do several properties, including a pub, in Greenwich. He also negotiated the lease on vacant rooms in the Royal Exchange which Lloyd's occupied from 1774 and where it remained until it moved to Leadenhall Street in 1928.

Fortunes and Misfortunes of War

The move to the Royal Exchange followed the end of the Seven Years' War with France, which ended in 1763 and left Great Britain in control of India and North America. Trade flourished with both of these and with it manifold opportunities for marine insurance. However, the successful war against France was soon followed by the American War of Independence and in August 1780

Lloyd's suffered one of its greatest blows when fifty-five British merchant ships were captured by the combined French and Spanish fleets who were supporting the American rebels. As John Walter, founding editor of *The Times* and himself a Lloyd's underwriter, wrote of the disaster, he was, 'weighed down in common with about half those who were engaged [as underwriters] by the host of foes this nation had to combat in the American War'. The disaster led, like those of the 1980s, to a great deal of litigation on the part of what one longstanding underwriter disapprovingly described as, 'Tradesmen, Shopkeepers etc. lured by the golden but delusive bait of Premiums' so that 'no less than 4 or 5 Attorneys were observed daily' at Lloyd's.

A New Home, with a Bell

Despite this setback the market quickly recovered so that between the time of the move to the Royal Exchange in 1774 and Napoleon's first abdication in 1814 the number of underwriters grew from 71 to 2,150. On 2 April 1800, in recognition that not all those hanging around the underwriting room were the most desirable characters, a resolution was passed restricting membership to applicants who were approved by the committee and who paid a subscription of £15. The Napoleonic Wars proved very profitable for Lloyd's as insurance premiums rose, shipping traffic increased and the ascendancy of the Royal Navy after the battle of Trafalgar ensured that many of the dangers to shipping (reflected in the high premiums) were more feared than real. The end of the wars was followed by a quieter but reasonably prosperous period, interrupted when the Royal Exchange was destroyed in a fire in 1838. The old building had seen better days and the underwriting room was described by the German princeling Puckler Muskau in 1826 as, 'the dirtiest place of the kind in London, which exhibits few traces of the millions daily exchanged in it'.

When the new Exchange opened in 1855 the underwriting room was praised for its 'elegant soap dishes, the spotless napkins, the china basins, the ivory-tipped cocks for the supply of hot and cold water' and the members marked their ascent into such superior premises by creating four categories of membership. Underwriting members, who alone could sign policies, and subscribers, who were brokers, were the heart of the market, the latter group bringing business to the former. Underwriters paid an entrance fee of £25 and each of these two groups also paid an annual membership subscription of four guineas (£4.20). Only underwriters and brokers were admitted to the underwriting room. Two further rooms, the Merchants' Room and the Captains' Room were available to gentlemen in those categories who paid an annual subscription of two guineas and one guinea respectively, the lower subscription for the captains reflecting the fact that, being often at sea, they were less able to take advantage of the

The Adam Room, where the Council of Lloyd's meets. (Wikicommons, Lloyd's of London picture)

facility. These rooms did, however, encourage potential sources of business to frequent the market. And, from 1859, the Underwriting Room accommodated the *Lutine* Bell, which has followed Lloyd's to each of its later homes and come to symbolise all the Lloyd's represents.

The *Lutine* Bell

This bell came from a French frigate, one of fifty-three captured by Lord Hood at Toulon in 1793. The Royal Navy used the *Lutine* ('the Sprite') to bombard the French artillery batteries commanded by the young Napoleon Bonaparte. In 1799 the *Lutine* sank off the coast of Holland together with all but one of her passengers and crew. The cargo, consisting of £1.2 million of gold and silver for banks in Hamburg, was insured by Lloyd's, which settled the claim in full and set about trying to recover the bullion. Attempts at salvage continued for over a century and some bullion and coins were recovered though much remains at the bottom of the North Sea. The ship's bell, engraved ST JEAN _ 1779 was recovered in 1858 and was brought to Lloyd's. No one knows why the name on the bell is not that of the ship. It was rung once to announce the late arrival and possible loss of a ship and twice to announce its return, this practice being adopted so that every member of the market would receive such critical news simultaneously and thereby eliminate any advantage gained from privileged information. During the Second World War, despite the claims of the Nazi propagandist Lord Haw Haw (William Joyce) that the bell was rung continuously to mark the loss of British ships it was in fact rung only once, to signify the sinking of the *Bismarck*. It has

The Lutine Bell at Lloyd's. (Lloyd's website)

developed a crack and was last rung to indicate the return of a ship in 1989. It is also rung when a member of the royal family dies and on such occasions as the 9/11 disaster, the Asian tsunami, the London bombings of July 2005 and to mark the end of the Lloyd's crisis of the 1980s and 1990s, as described below. It is also rung at the beginning and end of the two minutes silence on Armistice Day. Lloyd's also has a chair and table made from the rudder of the *Lutine*.

Early Scandals

In 1870 a major 'insider trading scandal' occurred involving a Liverpool ship-owner called Forwood who was also a Lloyd's underwriter. A rumour in the press that one of Forwood's ships, the *Venezuelan*, was severely damaged and possibly lost was known by its owner to be untrue since Forwood had received a reassuring message from the vessel's captain. Forwood asked his London agent to write a policy for £1,000 on which he duly made a substantial profit at the expense of others. When this sharp practice became known the committee attempted to expel Forwood from the market but learned from the Lord Chancellor, to whom Forwood had appealed, that it did not have the power to do so. The result was the Lloyd's Act of 1871 which turned the Society of Lloyd's into a corporation with clearly defined powers of discipline and specified that only an underwriting member could sign a Lloyd's policy – long a convention but now enshrined in law. This was another step along the road from private club to regulated market. It did not put an end to abuses. In 1902 an underwriter called Burnand who also ran a travel agency had diverted some premiums into his travel company and used the money to purchase seats for the forthcoming coronation of Edward VII. When the ceremony was postponed for two months because of the king's operation for suspected appendicitis Burnand's company failed, taking with it several underwriters. Burnand was duly expelled.

'Report me to Lloyd's'

The years that followed marked a number of advances in the way that Lloyd's managed its business. Agents had long been appointed in the world's key ports who could relay intelligence to keep the market informed of shipping movements, losses, commodity prices and other matters which would influence policies. The system had been introduced in the early nineteenth century under the leadership of Joseph Marryat whose son, Captain Frederick Marryat, himself introduced some novel procedures for signalling between ship and shore. He later took up a career as a writer of adventure stories, especially for children, such as *Masterman Ready*, written in 1841. Sir Henry Hozier, secretary of Lloyd's from 1874 to 1906 and father of Clementine, future wife of Winston Churchill, added a system of coastal signalling stations that relayed intelligence to Lloyd's and gave it unrivalled information about shipping movements and fortunes. One of his stations survives in the era of radio and the internet. It is operated by the Royal Navy at Gibraltar and ships entering and leaving the Mediterranean still send it the signal 'Report me to Lloyd's'.

New Risks, New Markets

At about the same time an underwriter called Cuthbert Heath, who became a member of Lloyd's with a loan of £7,000 from his father, began to take on non-marine risks including fire, burglary and earthquakes while he also devised the concept of credit insurance to protect companies against default-ing debtors. His innovations first attracted suspicion and hostility from established Lloyd's syndicates but they had the beneficial effect of taking the organisation into new markets at a time when shipping was undergoing one of its periodic recessions. In 1904 Lloyd's, in keeping with its growing reputa-tion for innovation, wrote the first policy for a car which, in the absence of any other vocabulary, was described as 'a ship navigating on land' and in 1911 it added its first aviation policy to coincide with the first London to Manchester flight. In the years that followed, Lloyd's became famous for taking on risks that others would not touch, from film stars' legs to a comedian's teeth and a cricketer's moustache. In 1906 Lloyd's strengthened its reputation by being the first organisation to pay out claims for the San Francisco earthquake when Cuthbert Heath ordered, 'pay all our policy holders in full irrespective of the terms of their policies'. This cost Lloyd's about $100 million (£25 million at the time) but as other insurers failed or claimed that their policies did not cover earthquakes Heath's decision earned Lloyd's an unrivalled reputation for probity in accordance with the principle of *Uberrima Fides*, or 'Utmost Good Faith', first pronounced by Lord Chief Justice Mansfield in 1766 in connection with insurance contracts. Lloyd's had adopted the expression as its code of behaviour.

In 1908 a campaign in *The Times* prompted by Sidney Boulton, a member of the Committee of Lloyd's, argued for a much more rigorous process of auditing the accounts of syndicates. It reminded its readers that a syndicate could have a premium income of a million pounds a year underwritten by a multitude of Lloyd's names, these being individuals who deposited £5,000 each and had little idea of what happened to the premium income – how much went to pay out for risks, how much to the agents who underwrote them and how much in payments to the names themselves. The committee, dominated by the assertive Cuthbert Heath, adopted a more rigorous system of auditing, another step towards full accountability.

Honouring A Bargain, Even With The Enemy

In 1911, in the face of growing anxiety about the power and ambitions of the Kaiser's Germany, the Committee of Imperial Defence instigated an enquiry into the commercial and financial repercussions of a conflict between the two nations. A member of the committee, the Earl of Desart, questioned a number of City grandees to this end. One of those who gave evidence was a leading Lloyd's underwriter called Robert Ogilvie who was questioned about what his view would be if, in the event of war, a German ship, insured at Lloyd's, were to be captured and destroyed by the Royal Navy. Ogilvie assured the earl that Lloyd's would pay up, which brought forth the reply, 'just consider the meaning of that'. To this Ogilvie responded that his answer was, 'rather governed, from our point of view, by the honourable carrying out of our bargain'. However, before the onset of war, on 15 April 1912, Lloyd's faced one of its sternest tests when the 'unsinkable' *Titanic* struck an iceberg in the North Atlantic, all but one of the major underwriters having insured the ship. The exception was (later Sir) Edward Mountain (1872–1948), the Angerstein of his day, with a reputation for shrewd judgement that helped him to found Eagle Star Insurance.

More Names Wanted

At the start of the twentieth century about half of the world's marine insurance was undertaken through Lloyd's as well as an increasing volume of other kinds of insurance. It was by some distance the dominant force in the world's insurance market and following the San Francisco earthquake its reputation was at its height. Later in the century it fell from grace as a result of incompetence, some corrupt practices and what became known as a 'democratic deficit' in which market 'insiders' (those names who worked in Lloyd's itself) were thought to profit at the expense of external names who were recruited in growing numbers from the 1970s onwards. Four groups of people are critical to an understanding of the problems that arose. Lloyd's Members' Agents work on behalf of the 'names' whose money actually underwrites the risks and who could forfeit all their assets if the risks they were underwriting went badly wrong. The Members' Agents choose the Lloyd's syndicates in which they recommend their names to invest. Some syndicates specialise in certain types of insurance (shipping, motor cars, household, marine etc.) and some spread themselves across many markets. The Managing Agents control the syndicates, admit new names to their registers and decide which specific risks to underwrite. Until the late nineteenth century many syndicates consisted of a handful of names – perhaps that of the managing agent himself and a few friends and relatives. In the twentieth century syndicates could have thousands of names, most of them unknown to the managing agent. Finally Lloyd's brokers bring the risks to the market on behalf of clients (motorists, householders etc.) and try to get the best deal they can for them in return for a commission. It was to be suggested that the misfortunes which struck down, and in some cases ruined, some names later in the century were caused by the fact that some Members' Agents and Managing Agents placed less risky and more profitable business with market insiders, leaving the less attractive risks to outside names. This became more critical as the number of external names increased and was to become a major source of grievance and controversy as Lloyd's continued to have many of the characteristics of a private club.

Mini-Names

In September 1965 Hurricane Betsy struck the Gulf of Mexico, causing damage to the offshore oil industry and triggering a series of events that were to transform Lloyd's amidst much controversy over the next thirty years. Its immediate effect was to bring about two years of losses at Lloyd's so that many names (whose numbers had grown from 2,000 to more than 6,000 since the Second World War) were writing cheques rather than receiving payments in 1966–67. Many of them, disillusioned, left the market, which reduced its capacity at a time when other insurers, many from the United States, were entering the London market. Lord Cromer, former governor of the Bank of England, was therefore asked to produce a report on Lloyd's, which resulted in the Cromer Report, published in 1969. This recommended that underwriting be made more attractive to external names who did not work in the market, in order to broaden its capital base and hence its capacity for taking on more business. Cromer also recommended that the financial requirements to become a name be reduced to a level at which it would be within the means of reasonably prosperous middle-class professionals like lawyers, doctors and accountants rather than the landed gentry. The membership fee for joining was reduced from £75,000 to £50,000 and this could be in the form of a house or flat that the name could continue to occupy while pledging it to Lloyd's. A minimum deposit of £35,000 would enable the new name to underwrite risks of ten times that amount – £350,000. For working names, those employed in the market, the membership fee was £3,000 and the minimum deposit £15,000.

These new 'cut price' investors become known as Mini-Names and the report also drew attention to the fact that a conflict of interest could arise between those underwriters who were working within the market and those who were merely investors. The name, as the report observed, had no control over the judgement of the underwriters taking risks on his behalf, yet in the words of the report, 'the Name is liable to the last penny of his possessions to meet underwriting losses'. Nothing was done to remedy this conflict of interest and it became an issue two decades later when claims related to asbestosis threatened some names with bankruptcy. The sums have been increased since the Cromer recommendations so that a Lloyd's name now needs £600,000, of which £200,000 is needed to buy into a syndicate and £400,000, in liquid assets like cash deposits, shares and bonds is deposited with Lloyd's and may be called upon to meet claims. However, any interest or dividends earned on the deposits is still paid to the name and the deposits can underwrite two and a half times the value of the deposit. So the £400,000 will earn its dividends *plus* any profit on £1 million of insurance that is underwritten.

In the 1970s the number of outside names almost tripled from fewer than 5,000 to almost 14,000 and by the 1980s it exceeded 32,000, a process encouraged by the fact that profits in Lloyd's could be presented for tax purposes as capital gains. At a time when the top tax rate on earned income was 83 per cent and that on investment 98 per cent, while capital gains tax stood at only 40 per cent this was a reason for many reasonably prosperous people with little understanding of the market to become external names. The other attractions remained: the fact that deposits continue to earn interest and dividends for the name while also working to earn further profits from underwriting. This is a very attractive proposition as long as things go reasonably well and even in a poor year, with losses, it is not bad. But very bad times indeed lay just ahead.

An Earthquake, an Oil Spill and Asbestos

In the 1980s a series of court judgements in the United States made substantial awards to people who had suffered from exposure to asbestos and other hazards, the compensation being at a level far beyond any provision that Lloyd's had made for policies which in some cases dated back to the 1940s. In comparison with the asbestos and other pollution claims, disasters like the 1988 Exxon Valdez oil spill and the 1989 San Francisco earthquake were modest in their effects. In 1988 Lloyd's announced a loss of £510 million, the biggest in its history but, as further unfavourable judgements followed, this loss was dwarfed, with losses reaching almost £9 billion over the next four years. The way in which Lloyd's syndicates were organised was such that members joining a syndicate in the 1980s could find themselves liable for claims that had arisen from policies written in the distant past – in some cases before they were born. These were known as long tail claims. The rapid increase in external names in the 1970s meant that many of those penalised in this way were relative newcomers to the market, outsiders to whom it came as a most unwelcome surprise that, far from profiting from their status as a Lloyd's name they were threatened with ruin. There followed allegations that, as the full extent of hazard-related liabilities become clear, Lloyd's insiders, backed by the Cromer report, had actively followed a policy of 'recruit to dilute', drawing in a multitude of new, unsuspecting outside names to share the mounting losses. Some cases were tragic including that of a lady who had worked for twenty-five years as an administrator for a Lloyd's broker. In 1979 she was made a name as a reward for her service by colleagues who, though well intentioned, were in effect giving her a ticket to penury. Her £35,000 gift led to losses that swiftly approached £100,000 and left her in despair. A retired pharmacist from Gloucestershire scraped together the money he needed to become a name with a view to providing a reasonable enhance-ment to his pension and was placed on syndicates heavily exposed to asbestos, pollution and other catastrophic risks. Losses amounting to £2 million fol-lowed, leading to a retirement beset by anxiety and privation. Some names reported that they dreaded opening the post for fear that it would contain yet more demands for money and some suicides followed the endless losses.

'Change the wealth of nations [and] bankrupt Lloyd's'

Conspiracy theories abounded, helped by the fact that not all syndicates were affected, with those confining their activities to mundane activities like motor, household and shipping continuing to return steady profits. One account held that the asbestos disaster had been discussed during a golf tour-nament in Surrey when it was suggested by one underwriter to another that asbestos claims would 'change the wealth of nations [and] bankrupt Lloyd's of London'. Other claims were more soundly based. In the early 1980s a secret Bank of England enquiry into Lloyd's warned of enormous losses which could engulf Lloyd's itself and affect banks which had loaned money to Lloyd's syn-dicates. At this time a new Lloyd's Bill was making its way through Parliament that attracted some surprising comments from opposite sides of the house. A proposal to give Lloyd's immunity from civil actions was opposed by a Conservative MP who was a lawyer and could not understand why 'a body that has been negligent [should] be protected from its own negligence' while Michael Meacher, the Labour spokesman, felt that to deny it such immunity would restrict its ability to regulate the market. Further problems emerged when Ian Hay Davison, formerly with the accountants Arthur Anderson, became Lloyd's Chief Executive in 1983. He took on the task with some reluctance at the request of the governor of the Bank of England, Gordon Richardson, and discovered that, far from the problem lying with a few rotten apples, 'It was the barrel itself that was in some danger of being tainted, in the sense that the corruption and malpractices touched a number of members of the committee – the regulating body – as well as ordinary underwriters'. At a council meeting to discuss the next chairman of Lloyd's to replace Sir Peter Green, Davison made no friends by observing that the Inland Revenue was investigating many of the candidates for the role, because of their possible association with offshore funds. Many were relieved when he resigned.

A New Home but *Uberrima Fides* is Left Behind

In 1986 Lloyd's briefly attracted more favourable notices when it moved to the new Lloyd's building designed by Richard Rogers, having previously occupied premises in the Royal Exchange, Leadenhall Street and Lime Street. This new building is close to the former home of Lloyd's on Lime Street and stands on the site of the former Leadenhall Street building, an arch of which was actually incorporated into the new structure. This is the famous 'Inside Out' building, reminiscent of the architect's Pompidou centre in Paris, with services such as heating, lifts, ventilation and water pipes visible on the exterior of the structure. In the new edition of Nikolaus Pevsner's *Buildings of England* the building was described as, 'the most consistently innovative building the City has seen since Soane's Bank of England' though one underwriter lamented, 'we started off in a coffee-house and finished up in a coffee percolator'.

Into the melee of losses, conspiracy theories and accusations of bad faith, far from *Uberrima Fides*, was tossed in 1987 the Neill Report. Sir Patrick Neill, QC, vice-chancellor of Oxford University, had been asked to chair a committee to examine the regulation of the market. The report drew attention to the conflict of interest that had always existed between market insiders (the agents and names working within Lloyd's); and the external names whose numbers had increased so much since the Cromer report had opened up the market to new names and the capital they brought with them. The report, quoting an earlier report into a scandal involving a Lloyd's syndicate, noted that:

> Many members of the Lloyd's community in senior positions were not even vaguely aware of the legal obligations upon agents to act at all times in the best interests of their principals, [i.e. their names] not to make secret profits at their principals' expense and to disclose fully all matters affecting their relationship with their principals.

The practice had developed amongst some managing agents of diverting the most attractive business to baby syndicates consisting of favoured names, most of whom worked within Lloyd's itself, while the external names took on the more doubtful risks, similar in some ways to the insider trading which bedevilled the stock market. One syndicate, in 1981, produced a profit of 385 per cent for its three members and in the same year another syndicate, with seven members, returned 270 per cent while names on other syndicates faced ruinous losses. Sir Patrick Neill recommended that this problem be addressed by ensuring that the governing council of Lloyd's should have a majority of outside members. This ensured that the 'insiders' could no longer order the conduct of the market in their own interests but many external names must have felt that, for many years, the principle of *Uberrima Fides* had not applied to the market's dealings with them. The days of the private club, trusted to regulate its own affairs, were swiftly drawing to a close in face of the gathering storm.

'Staggering failings and incompetence'

It was estimated that 10,000 underwriting names, approaching a third of the total number, lost potentially ruinous sums of money and many others incurred uncomfortable losses. Individual names had lost sums between £120,000 and £5 million, many having to sell homes and businesses to meet their liabilities. Losers included Princess Michael of Kent, Camilla Parker-Bowles, Jeffrey Archer, Sir Edward Heath, Frances Shand-Kydd (mother of Diana Princess of Wales), the Wimbledon champion Virginia Wade and the popular former boxer Henry Cooper who was obliged to sell some of his sporting trophies to cover his losses. About 95 per cent each paid £100,000 to Lloyd's to settle the claims but a small group took the case to court, arguing in effect that Lloyd's had defrauded them. They were led by a retired fine art dealer, Sir William Jaffray, their case being that Lloyd's had recruited them knowing of the forthcoming avalanche of claims. On 3 November 2000, in the High Court, Mr Justice Cresswell dismissed the claim that Lloyd's had acted knowingly in recruiting names to share the losses but pronounced that the names were the 'innocent victims ... of staggering failings and incompetence'. He added that, 'the answer to the question whether there was in existence a rigorous system of auditing which involved the making of a reasonable estimate of outstanding liabilities, including unknown and un-noted losses, is 'no'".

'Who wants to be a member of Lloyd's ... I don't'

Some of the names who faced bankruptcy applied to the Lloyd's hardship committee, chaired by Dr Mary Archer, a member of the Council of Lloyd's. The committee required applicants to make over all their assets to Lloyd's in return for which they would be allowed to retain a modest home (£150,000, quite a pleasant home in the 1990s) and an annual income of £11,600 for a single person or £17,600 for a married couple. The terms were designed to be better than bankruptcy but were hardly attractive to people accustomed to an affluent lifestyle. It was later claimed that at a gathering of underwriters Dr Archer, a fine singer, had given a rendering of 'Who Wants to be a Millionaire', sung by Frank Sinatra in the 1950s film *High Society*, but to different words:

> Who wants to be a member of Lloyd's ... I don't

There is no record of the reception given by the audience.

In 1993 the chairman of Lloyd's Council, Sir David Rowland, set in motion a plan which eventually returned the market to health. The number of names fell to fewer than 10,000 in the 1990s, some leaving through bankruptcy or resort to the hardship fund and others, more fortunate, leaving voluntarily though disillusioned by the incompetence and malpractice which they felt had been visited upon them. In 1993 Lloyd's created a reinsurer called Equitas, which would assume all outstanding liabilities prior to that date. It had capital of £859 million provided by surviving members and Lloyd's brokers. For the first time since Edward Lloyd opened his coffee shop in Tower Street in 1688, corporations were admitted to membership. Their corporate status limited their liability but their financial resources greatly increased the financial base of the market. Moreover the liabilities of individual names were limited to a proportion (80 per cent) of premium income, any excess being met by a reserve fund met by annual membership fees. The possibility of loss was thus still substantial but not without limit. Finally, the hardship fund was wound up and after many bitter court battles a settlement was reached with litigating names.

Thrice Tolls the Bell

In the summer of 1996 David Rowland rang the *Lutine* Bell three times, the first time that this has happened and, it is hoped, the last. The first ring marked the sufferings of names who had borne losses totalling more than £8 billion; the second the successful implementation of the recovery plan; and the third the start of work to restore Lloyd's reputation as a centre of excellence and international competitiveness. A line had been drawn under the disasters of the previous twenty years, Lloyd's had returned to profitability and it could breathe again. By the dawn of the new millennium 80 per cent of Lloyd's capital was provided by corporate members and from 2001 the market was regulated by the Financial Services Authority, not by Lloyd's itself, thereby diminishing the dangers of 'insider trading' which had, in the view of many, bedevilled the recent past. Lloyd's had completed its journey from private club to a fully regulated corporate body with proper concerns for its external investors.

In 2001, fifteen years after it moved to its new home, Lloyd's was given the opportunity to restore its reputation in circumstances reminiscent of those surrounding the San Francisco earthquake of 1906 when it had paid claims in full. Following the attack on the World Trade Centre on 11 September, Lloyd's, in the words of the US Treasury Secretary John Snow, 'Stepped up to the plate' and met its obligations. It continues to have a global influence and in 2007 opened a reinsurance operation in Shanghai to serve China's fast-growing market. Its capital base, which in 1990 at the height of its troubles stood at £18 billion, now exceeds £70 billion. In 2012, Aon, the world's largest insurance broker, moved its headquarters from Chicago to London to be close to the centre of the world's insurance market. Lloyd's reputation for innovation in insurance continues and those who wish to insure against risks that conventional insurance companies will not cover continue to resort to Lloyd's. Their syndicates have covered:

The legs of Betty Grable, Brooke Shields and Tina Turner

The distinctive walrus moustache of Australian cricketer Merv Hughes

The taste buds of food critic Egon Ronay

Singer Whitney Houston's vocal chords

The motor cars in the carpools involved in the 1955 Montgomery Bus Boycott which set off the civil rights movement in the USA: no US insurer would touch them

Ken Dodd's teeth

A prize of £1 million offered by a Scotch whisky company for catching the Loch Ness Monster. In the event of the prize being claimed the monster would become the property of the underwriters. The prize has yet to be claimed so at present the underwriters do not have to worry about where they will keep the monster.

A 'virtual tour' of Lloyd's may be undertaken by visiting the website at www. lloyds.com. If you wish to visit the building itself then call 0207 327 1000; or email: enquiries@lloyds.com.

15

Covent Garden

In 1985 it was revealed that the area now known as Covent Garden had a longer history than previously realised. It had long been recognised that the road to the south of the area, then running along the banks of the Thames and known as the river's Strand, had been the early stage of a Roman road known as Iter VII (route 7) leading to the important Roman settlement of Silchester near the present site of Reading.

The Strand

The Strand is so called because until the 1860s the River Thames was much wider than it is now. The river lapped the gardens of the great palaces which lay on the south side of the Strand such as the Savoy, the home of John of Gaunt, Essex House and Northumberland House. When Sir Joseph Bazalgette (1819–91) built the Victoria Embankment from Westminster Bridge to Blackfriars Bridge to accommodate his great low-level sewer which protected the Thames from London's waste, he reclaimed 42 acres of land from the river and thereby distanced the Strand from the river to which it owed its name. The name nevertheless remained.

It had been assumed that the area north of the Strand had been fields used for grazing and the cultivation of crops but, from 1985, excavations revealed a substantial Anglo-Saxon settlement known as Lundenwic, or 'London trading town'. It was known to the Venerable Bede (673–735) who described it as, 'a trading centre for many nations who visit it by land and sea' but was long forgotten after Alfred the Great moved the community to within the walls of the City itself for its better protection. The 1985 excavations exposed a substantial settlement which had once stretched from the present site of Trafalgar Square to the Aldwych ('Old Market Place') where Alfred had granted the Danes a trading post after defeating them in May 878 and making peace with their king, Guthrum.

A Convent Garden

By 1200 the former trading settlement had reverted to agricultural use and had been acquired by Westminster Abbey as arable land for use as an orchard. It became known as 'the garden of the Abbey and Convent' the last word being shortened to 'Covent' which gave the area its later name 'Covent Garden'. The abbey and convent succumbed to Henry VIII's dissolution of the monasteries and in 1552 Henry's son and successor, Edward VI, granted it to John Russell, the first Earl of Bedford whose successors (later becoming Dukes of Bedford) owned much of the land to the north of the Strand including Bloomsbury, itself north of Covent Garden. The estate granted by Edward VI was bounded by St Martin's Lane in the west, Drury Lane in the east, Long Acre in the north and the Strand in the south. The fourth earl commissioned Inigo Jones (1573–1652) to lay out the Covent Garden area with fine buildings. Inigo Jones, the son of a Welsh Catholic clothworker, may have owed his unusual Christian name to Basque ancestry (Ynigo, Latinised

Covent Garden hustings, 1808, an election address drawing a large crowd, Inigo Jones's St Paul's church in the background. (Wikimedia Commons, public domain)

to Ignatius). In 1613 he was appointed Surveyor of the King's Works by James I and a visit to Italy shortly afterwards introduced him to the classical disciplines of architecture then prevalent in Italy but little-known in England. The earl probably gave the work to Inigo Jones because, as the king's surveyor, Jones was responsible for ensuring that the regulations governing new buildings were observed. James I had placed severe restrictions on building within the Covent Garden area and by employing Inigo Jones to carry out the work the earl no doubt surmised that he would have few difficulties with the king's surveyor! A little local difficulty with James's son and successor Charles I was settled by the payment of £4,000 to that perpetually impecunious monarch.

'The finest barn in Europe'

The earl chose well. Inigo Jones became the first exponent of the classical style in England and followed its principles both in the Banqueting Hall in Whitehall and in his designs for Covent Garden with its Italianate arcaded square of fine houses, soon referred to by the novel Italian word 'piazza'. The earl informed his architect that he wanted him to incorporate a church at minimum cost, little more than a barn, and Jones answered that he would have 'the finest barn in Europe', the resulting St Paul's church being the first truly classical church in England, a style later adopted by Christopher Wren in his first commission, the Chapel of Pembroke College, Cambridge and in his London churches following the Great Fire of 1665. The interior was damaged by fire in 1795 but the exterior remains faithful to Jones's design and its fine portico is the dominant feature of the west side of the market. It is known as 'the actors' church' because of the strong associations of the area with the acting profession. The church is all that remains of Inigo Jones's design but the piazza-like layout of the later buildings by Charles Fowler echoes that which was envisaged by Jones.

The church was consecrated in 1638 and the houses were occupied by wealthy and fashionable residents but in the 1650s a market developed on the southern part of the square. The market is first mentioned in a protest by the Aldermen of the City of London in 1649 since Edward III had, in 1328, given the City Corporation a monopoly over the establishment of markets within a 7-mile radius. Their protest was unavailing and by 1657 the churchwardens of St Paul's church were paying 30s for repainting some benches in 'the Merkett place'. The market expanded when the Great Fire of 1665 destroyed many of the City's markets and in 1670 its existence was first officially recognised by a royal charter granting the earl the right to hold a market for fruit, flowers, roots and herbs every day except Sundays and Christmas Day and to collect tolls from the traders. The first tenants traded from premises that were little more than garden sheds in the piazza but by 1748 these had been replaced by more substantial buildings with cellars which still comprise part of the vaults beneath the present market buildings.

'All the prostitutes in the kingdom'

The noise, traffic and waste generated by the market encouraged the wealthy to move out, to be swiftly replaced by coffee houses, taverns, prostitutes, brothels, Turkish baths of dubious quality and theatres. In 1776 one visitor reported, 'One would imagine that all the prostitutes in the kingdom had pitched upon this blessed neighbourhood for a place of general rendezvous'. And actors, of course, were regarded as little better than prostitutes. The Theatre Royal in nearby Drury Lane, London's oldest continuously used theatre, opened in 1663, and the (later Royal) Opera House opened as a theatre in 1732. The present buildings date from the nineteenth century following fires which destroyed both on more than one occasion. They are both huge, each seating more than 2,000 people. There were also publishers at a time when this activity was often associated with subversive pamphlets. By the eighteenth century Covent Garden had acquired the sort of reputation associated with the seedier parts of Soho in a later century and it was not by chance that the novelist Henry Fielding and his brother John set up their incorruptible Bow Street Magistrates' Court and Bow Street Runners in the Covent Garden area. Henry Fielding was so impressed by the hordes of prostitutes in the area that he called the piazza, 'The Great Square of Venus'.

Henry Fielding (1707–54)

Fielding was appointed Justice of the Peace for Middlesex in 1747, having made his name as a playwright, novelist (*Tom Jones*) and supporter of the Tory government. He received his salary of £200 a year from the Secret Service fund and abandoned the corrupt practices associated with 'thief-takers' like Jonathan Wilde (see page 60) earlier in the century. He appointed six honest constables who later became known as the Bow Street Runners. His brother John, after Henry's death, added mounted patrols. He managed to rid Covent Garden area of the lawless gangs who dominated the area and after one particularly ferocious battle in 1753, when seven gang leaders were captured, the *Public Advertiser* reported that, 'since the apprehending of the Great Gang of Cut-Throats not a dangerous blow, shot or wound has been given either in roads or streets'. Fielding died in Lisbon in 1754 but his work at Bow Street formed the model for the

Metropolitan Police established by Robert Peel in 1829. Bow Street Magistrates' Court closed in 2006. The nearby Bow Street Police Station, one of London's first, did not adopt the blue lamps associated with police stations when these were introduced in 1861. Instead the station was unique in having a white lamp. This was to avoid offending Queen Victoria during her visits to the Opera House since the blue lamps reminded her of the Blue Room at Windsor in which her husband Prince Albert had died in 1861.

The colourful nature of the area that was eventually to accommodate London's principal fruit and vegetable market may be deduced by a publication called *Harris's List of Covent Garden Ladies* which modestly described itself as an 'essential guide and accessory for any serious gentleman of pleasure' published annually from 1757 to 1795.

Covent Garden Market, 2008. (Wikimedia Commons, Josep Renalias)

A New Market

Despite the efforts of the Fieldings the Covent Garden area's theatrical associations continued to give it a rather louche reputation and the Duke of Bedford was becoming increasingly frustrated by the wiles of traders who exploited loopholes in market regulations to reduce the tolls they paid for trading. In 1827 the government paid the duke £29,000 for some land that it needed to widen the Strand and in 1830 he commissioned the architect

Charles Fowler to rebuild the market in its entirety. The duke had been impressed by Fowler's designs for Hungerford Market, on the present site of Charing Cross Station (see page 161). Fowler built the present market hall to replace the tumbledown sheds and hovels which had previously accommodated the traders. Three parallel ranges of shops, fronted by colonnades, with terraces above, accommodated both wholesale and retail traders. Heated conservatories were available for the more delicate plants and ample space was left between the shops for moving, parking and unloading carts. Granite was used to face those parts of the building which would be vulnerable to collisions by carts. The work was carried out by the builder William Cubitt, his tender price of £34,850 falling far short of the eventual cost of almost £70,000, a price which placed considerable strains upon the duke's finances.

William Cubitt (1791–1863)

Cubitt was one of three brothers who built much of Victorian London. Besides Covent Garden William built Cubitt Town on the Isle of Dogs and his younger brother Lewis (1799–1883) built King's Cross Station and the Great Northern Hotel. The most active brother was Thomas Cubitt (1788–1855) who built much of Belgravia, Bloomsbury, Pimlico, Clapham and rebuilt Osborne House for Queen Victoria who greatly admired her 'favourite builder'. Thomas left the longest will on record at 386 pages. The Duchess of Cornwall is one of his descendants.

The glass roof was added in the 1870s and the flower market, now occupied by London's Transport Museum, soon followed. It was the haunt of Eliza Doolittle and the scene of her encounter with Professor Henry Higgins in George Bernard Shaw's *Pygmalion*, later to become the 1950s musical *My Fair Lady*. The Floral Hall in the north-east corner of the site was conceived by the manager of the Opera House, Frederick Gye, and was built after the Opera House burned down in 1856. Its fine arched glass roof and cast-iron columns were absorbed into the Opera House during the redevelopment of the 1990s and its portico was transferred to Borough Market in Southwark (see page 148).

By the 1880s the market was severely overcrowded, with over 700 firms or individuals paying tolls to twelve market officials operating on behalf of the Bedford estate, assisted by seven constables hired from the Metropolitan Police. A thousand porters were paid a weekly wage of between 30s and 45s, their numbers sometimes being swollen by the army of unemployed labourers who walked the streets in search of work. The market gradually expanded from the piazza, which it had long dominated and stretched as far north as Seven Dials, London's most notorious slum, on the site now occupied by

Centre Point near Tottenham Court Road underground station. In the 1880s the market was the target of criticism in the press led by *Punch* which described the 'Mud-salad market' as a disgrace to London and 'a Leviathan nuisance'. The Duke of Bedford had for some time been trying to rid himself of the market and offered it both to the City Corporation and to the Metropolitan Board of Works which had been set up in 1856 as London's first Metropolitan authority outside the City itself and would eventually give way to the London County Council. Both bodies wisely declined the duke's offer, deterred by the troubles and criticism which beset the market.

Beechams' Pills Take Over

In 1913 the eleventh duke agreed to sell the Covent Garden Estate to a Member of Parliament called Harry Mallaby-Deeley who was also a property developer. He sold on his option to the Beecham family whose most celebrated member was the conductor Sir Thomas Beecham and who owed their wealth to Beechams' Pills. In 1962 they sold the market estate for £3,925,000 to the Greater London Council-owned Covent Garden Authority who set about confronting the traffic problems posed by a wholesale market employing 1,000 porters in one of London's busiest and most congested areas. The fruit and vegetable market was moved to Nine Elms, a former British Rail goods depot in Lambeth, in 1974.

Initial plans for the demolition of much of the Covent Garden area and its comprehensive redevelopment with hotels, boulevards and conference centres were greeted with cries of outrage and in 1973 the plans were forestalled when 250 buildings in the area were granted listed status, including Fowler's market buildings. More sympathetic restoration and redevelopment followed and in 1980 the market reopened with a multitude of restaurants, shops, museums and spas, the last reminiscent of the Turkish baths which once gave the area a bad name. Street performers audition with the landlords for a slot on the open space in front of Inigo Jones's St Paul's church, the last complete element of Jones's design. The Apple Market sells antiques, paintings and the hand-made products of craftsmen. The nearby streets continue to be populated with publishers, as in the eighteenth century, and bookshops as well as the Garrick Club, associated with actors and other entertainers. In 2006 many of the retail buildings were bought by a property company on a 150-year lease. They are let to the Covent Garden Area Trust which pays an annual rent to the trust of one red apple and a posy of flowers and protects the area from redevelopment.

Covent Garden Market, 2008. (Wikimedia Commons,Josep Renalias)

WHEN CAN I VISIT?

The market is open virtually every day except Christmas Day. Its website can be found at www.coventgardenlondon.com.

New Covent Garden Market

This market is a wholesale fruit, vegetable and flower market in Nine Elms Lane, Lambeth, London SW8 5BH. It can be visited by members of the public and is open from midnight to 6 a.m. (fruit and vegetable market) and 2 a.m. to 8 a.m. (flower market), Monday to Saturday. On Sundays the Nine Elms Sunday Market opens at 11 a.m. with, it is estimated, over 1,000 stalls selling every kind of product from clothing to power tools and 'designer' accessories. Bargains can probably be found but discerning shoppers should be aware that the provenance of much of the merchandise is by no means clear. The nearest stations are Vauxhall Network Rail and Vauxhall Underground.

16

The Markets of the East End

The 'East End' of London, now covered by the boroughs of Tower Hamlets and Hackney, has an exceptionally diverse range of markets, many of them ancient. Since they are within walking distance of one another they will be dealt with together. Depending upon where one begins the visit, the area is well served by underground stations at Liverpool Street, Bethnal Green, Whitechapel, Aldgate and Aldgate East.

Spitalfields

Just across the boundary of the City of London, close to Liverpool Street Station, is the magnificent Victorian building which housed the Spitalfields fruit, vegetable and flower market. The market began life in the thirteenth century as a market in a field on the fringe of the Square Mile. The strange name derives from the fact that the field belonged to the 'Hospital of St Mary without (i.e. outside) Bishopsgate' commonly known as St Mary Spittal which was founded in 1197 on the site of a Roman cemetery. It was one of the biggest hospitals in England and was dissolved by Henry VIII in 1539. The remains of the hospital and the cemetery were excavated in the 1990s. The Roman cemetery yielded urns of funeral ash containing coins bearing the images of Claudius (who conquered Britain) and his successors Nero, Vespasian and Trajan, indicating that the site must have been in use from the earliest period of the Roman occupation. By the time that John Stow was writing, about 1600, the area was becoming built up for he recorded that:

> Hogge Lane stretched North towards Saint Mary Spittle without Bishopsgate, and within these forty years had on both sides fair hedgerows of Elm trees, with Bridges and easy Stiles to pass over into the pleasant fields, very commodious for citizens therein to walk, shoot and otherwise

Christ Church Spitalfields, built by Hawksmoor to draw Huguenots to the Anglican faith. (Wikicommons, Eluveitie)

to recreate and refresh their dulled spirits in the sweet and wholesome air, which is now within a few years made a continual building throughout of Garden houses and small cottages.

In 1638 Charles I granted to the area a licence for the sale of flesh, poultry and vegetables though this activity seems to have lapsed during the Civil War which soon followed. In 1682 Charles II renewed the licence for a market to supply the growing population of the City, the area of the market being demarcated by Lamb Street to the north and Brushfield Street to the south. In the same year the king granted to John Balch, a silk weaver, the right to hold a market on Thursdays and Saturdays on or near Spital Square. John Balch was probably one of a large community of Huguenots, Protestant refugees from the persecutions of Louis XIV, which drove tens of thousands of Louis' former subjects into exile in the Netherlands and Great Britain, many of them settling in Spitalfields. In 1687 it was estimated that over 13,000 Huguenots were in Spitalfields and the surrounding area. Many of them had arrived with no possessions and £200,000 was raised to support them while they established themselves as silk weavers, creating an industry new to London. In the years that followed they built ten of their own chapels and the fine church of Christ Church, Spitalfields was built by Nicholas Hawksmoor in an attempt to draw the population into the Anglican church. One Huguenot chapel, La Patente, on the corner of Brick Lane and Fournier Street, became successively a Wesleyan chapel, a synagogue and is now a mosque, reflecting the changing immigrant population of the area. In the eighteenth century a number of fine terraced houses were built in Fournier Street to accommodate the wealthy master weavers and more modest dwellings for weavers in nearby Tenterground.

'Murder on an average once a month'

In the 1730s Irish weavers began to join the Huguenots, driven from Ireland by a decline in the demand for Irish linen and this, combined with cyclical depressions, led to protests and occasional riots, an Irish and a Huguenot weaver being hanged in Bethnal Green in 1769. As the silk industry declined in the nineteenth century the Huguenots moved out to be replaced by Jewish immigrants who brought tailoring and boot-making skills. However, by this time much of the area had deteriorated into a lawless slum and it was in Dorset Street, to the south of Spitalfields market, that Jack the Ripper claimed his first victim in 1888. In 1901 the *Daily Mail* described Dorset Street as, 'a place which boasts of an attempt at murder on an average once a month … Policemen go down it as a rule in pairs'. Another wrote, 'It was a street of whores … peopled by roaring, drunken, fighting-mad killers'. Dorset Street was renamed Duval Street in 1904 and no longer exists, its site lying beneath the former London Fruit and Wool Exchange between Crispin Street and White's Row.

As late as 1867 the poet Matthew Arnold (1822–88), wrote of the fate of impoverished silk weavers in Spitalfields in his poem *East London*:

> 'Twas August, and the fierce sun overhead
> Smote on the squalid streets of Bethnal Green,
> And the pale weaver, through his windows seen
> In Spitalfields looked twice dispirited.

Despite the area's deterioration the market itself continued to flourish though for two centuries the market traded from stalls and makeshift sheds, opening six days a week to meet the needs of the neighbouring City. In 1876 a former Spitalfields market porter called Robert Horner purchased a lease on some of the land and built the present Spitalfields market building, the first purpose-built structure on the site. In 1920 the City of London Corporation took over the market and operated it as it did Smithfield. For sixty years the market thrived but like Billingsgate and Covent Garden it was handicapped by poor road access and the traffic congestion became intolerable. In 1991 it moved to a larger site in Leyton as a wholesale market with a new market hall, cold storage facilities, ripening rooms and adequate parking for traders and customers. The Old Spitalfields Market, as it is now called, was at one time threatened by the expansion of the City as it sought extra office space beyond the Square Mile but it has been refurbished and extended by the City Corporation. It narrowly avoided becoming a home for the London International Financial Futures Exchange and, with its Norman Foster designed western extension it now comprises modern office buildings, restaurants, shops and the Traders' Market which offers arts and crafts products as well as fashion and food. The market is open seven days a week and the market square is especially popular on Sundays with a designers' market on the third Sunday of each month. The area has become popular with writers, broadcasters and artists, residents including Tracey Emin, Gilbert & George, Dan Cruickshank and the writer Jeanette Winterson who converted a fine but derelict Georgian house into an organic food shop, Verde's.

Petticoat Lane and Brick Lane

A short distance to the South of Spitalfields is Middlesex Street which, with the adjoining Wentworth Street, comprises the market known as Petticoat

Lane. It is open from Monday to Friday on Wentworth Street and on Sundays it overflows into Middlesex Street and often further afield with as many as 1,000 stalls. It is closed on Saturday, the Jewish Sabbath, in recognition of the large population of Jewish traders who were found there from the eighteenth century. By the early seventeenth century some dwellings had appeared in the area which had acquired a substantial Spanish population including the residence of the Spanish ambassador as well as a number of traders of second-hand clothing. It was also at this time that the name 'Peticote' Lane became attached to the road which had previously been known as Hogge's Lane because of the pigs that grazed there. The new name referred to the lace garments which had replaced the pigs. In about 1830, during the reign of William IV, the name was changed to Middlesex Street to mark the boundary between the City and Whitechapel. To the north of Middlesex Street is Strype Street which, in the late seventeenth century, was the childhood home of John Strype (see page 56) who in 1720 updated John Stow's *Survey of London* and thereby left us with an account of London as it began the rapid expansion which led to its becoming the largest and wealthiest city in the world the following century. Many of the Huguenots who came to London about 1700 settled in the area (as they did in nearby Spitalfields) and brought with them skills in the dying of cloth. The dyed cloth was hung out

Wentworth Street, the heart of Petticoat Lane. (geograph.org.uk, Robert Lamb)

to dry on Tenterhooks and the name survives in the name of a nearby street, Tenterground. The Huguenots were joined in the late nineteenth century by Jewish immigrants who also set up clothing businesses and the area rapidly became London's 'garment district' with a multitude of small workshops at every level, from mass-produced cheap work garments to made-to-measure clothing, including some tailors who made up suits for Savile Row.

The area was badly bombed in the Second World War and substantially rebuilt in the 1950s and 1960s. The market, however, continued to thrive though it was long unpopular with the authorities since until the 1930s it was not legally constituted and was notorious for petty crime and especially popular with pickpockets. Attempts to suppress it included such tactics as driving police cars and fire engines through the market with lights flashing and bells ringing to disrupt the traders. It is as popular as ever in the twenty-first century and bargains are to be had, especially for those who are prepared to barter, though it is wise to examine goods with some care. A friend of the writer purchased a suit there and found, when he got it home, that the trousers had a leg missing! Some careers have been launched in Petticoat Lane, notably that of the entrepreneur Alan Sugar who in his younger days had a stall in the market.

Brick Lane

The settlement of Bangladeshi immigrants in Brick Lane, a short distance to the east with its own market, further strengthened the reputation of the area as a place where bargains were to be found. The markets have their own distinct character. Both sell clothing though the Brick Lane market has a wider variety of other products, notably Bangladeshi cuisine which, in the view of many, has made it the curry capital of the West. Much of the Brick Lane market is in fact in the grounds of the former Truman Brewery towards the northern end of Brick Lane, close to the junction with Quaker Street. The Sunday Upmarket off Hanbury Street, which bisects Brick Lane, has artwork by such prominent street artists as the mysterious Banksy. This market accommodates such products as handmade jewellery, designer clothing, vintage clothing and vinyl records. It also has international cuisine of every description including Lithuanian and Caribbean cafes and restaurants. One stall specialises in Cuban and Soviet revolutionary art. The market used to have a more doubtful reputation as a market place for stolen bicycles but this faded following a crackdown by the Metropolitan Police in 2010–11 which produced over a hundred arrests. *Brick Lane* is the title of a book by Monica Ali, published in 2003, which celebrates the vibrant multicultural character of the area through the life of a young Bangladeshi woman living in Tower Hamlets.

Running east from close to the northern end of Brick Lane is Cheshire Street which is an extension of the Brick Lane market. At No. 73, Cheshire Street, is the Carpenters' Arms, a public house bought for their mother Violet by the gangster twins Ronnie and Reggie Kray who, according to legend, replaced the bar surface with a coffin lid. It was close to their home in Vallance Road and Reggie's funeral cortege passed the pub in October 2000. The pub is now in safer hands.

The best time to visit both markets is on Sunday, when they are at their busiest though Brick Lane, in particular, is also very active on Friday and Saturday.

The Blind Beggar

Those with a taste for the macabre may wish to take a few steps further to the south of Brick Lane to visit Whitechapel Market and, at No. 337, Whitechapel Road, seek some refreshment at the Blind Beggar public house outside which, in 1865, William Booth preached his first sermon which led to the formation of the Salvation Army. In March 1966, 101 years later, George Cornell was shot dead while sitting at the bar by Ronnie Kray, one of the notorious gangster twins. The present pub dates from 1894. A more salubrious experience is to be had to the east at Nos 77–82 Whitechapel High Street at the Whitechapel Art Gallery, opened in 1901. It has achieved a number of 'firsts' in major exhibitions of modern works including Picasso's Guernica in 1938 and major exhibitions by Jackson Pollock, Mark Rothko, David Hockney and Lucian Freud.

Columbia Road Flower Market: 'After my mother the most remarkable woman in the kingdom'

Columbia Market, which now trades only on Sundays, dates from 1869 when it was created by the Victorian philanthropist Angela Burdett Coutts (1814–1906). Described by the future Edward VII as, 'After my mother the most remarkable woman in the kingdom', her eccentricity was exceeded only by her great wealth. She was the daughter of the radical politician and MP Sir Francis Burdett who was gaoled for three months for denouncing the Peterloo Massacre of 1819, in which militia charged and killed a number of people in St Peter's Fields, Manchester, who were peacefully demonstrating in favour of Parliamentary reform. Frances Burdett married Sophia Coutts, descendant of the famous banking family, and in 1837 their daughter

The Blind Beggar, scene of Jack Cornell's murder by Ronnie Kray, now a more peaceful place. (Ewan Munro)

Columbia Road flower market, *Illustrated London News*, 1869. (Wikimedia Commons)

Angela became the wealthiest woman in England with a fortune of £1.8 million, though she would forfeit 60 per cent of this inheritance if she married a foreigner. She rejected a marriage proposal from the future Napoleon III of France and was herself rejected by the ageing and widowed Duke of Wellington. At the age of sixty-six, however, she married her twenty-nine-year-old American secretary, thereby losing much of her inheritance. Queen Victoria described the marriage as 'positively distressing and ridiculous' but it did nothing to circumscribe her circle of admirers and visitors to her St James's Square home included William Gladstone, Michael Faraday, Charles Babbage and Charles Dickens who dedicated *Martin Chuzzlewit* to her. When she died 30,000 people filed past her coffin.

Resurrection Men

Much of her philanthropy was directed towards the East End. She provided drinking fountains for the poor to obtain clean water free of charge, one of which survives in Victoria Park, Hackney and she also paid for the construction of model tenements at Nova Scotia gardens, Bethnal Green, in what had been one of the foulest slums in London known as the Jago. In 1831, with the aid of the newly established Metropolitan Police, the authorities revealed a series of crimes at No. 3, Nova Scotia Gardens, involving Resurrection

Columbia Road flower market, 2007. (Wikimedia Commons, Edward Betts)

Men who murdered individuals, often homeless people, so that their corpses could be sold for dissection to teaching hospitals. The most notorious was that of a young boy known as The Italian Boy who was abducted, drugged, drowned (so that there were no marks on his body) and offered for sale to King's College Hospital who informed the authorities of their suspicions. This led to the arrest, trial and execution of the two men involved, John Bishop and Thomas Williams. Such was the notoriety of the crime that the police opened the decrepit building for viewing, charging members of the public an admission fee. Much of its crumbling fabric was removed by the visitors as souvenirs and following its further deterioration Angela Burdett Coutts bought the land for Columbia market.

Her intention was to establish a covered food market which would rid the area of costermongers (barrow boys) and provide a source of fresh air to the local population as well as cheap and wholesome food. It opened in 1869; a fine Victorian Gothic edifice with space for 400 stalls and trading on Saturdays though this was soon switched to Sundays to accommodate the large population of Jewish traders. It cost £200,000 and its most distinctive feature was a fine clock tower which played a hymn tune every fifteen minutes. It never flourished as she intended. Plans to introduce a railway line to bring fresh fish to the market were never put into effect and the local costermongers persisted in trading in the open rather than in the market. Their barrows became a means by which the traders of Covent Garden and Spitalfields could dispose of the produce left after Saturday's trading at Columbia Road on Sundays.

In that form the market continues to thrive on Sundays from 8 a.m. to 2 p.m., traders arriving from 4 a.m. to set up their stalls. The market is now mostly devoted to horticulture, with cut flowers, shrubs, bulbs and bedding plants, many of the stalls being operated by descendants of those who were trading at the covered market in its earliest days. To these have since been added fresh bread, cheese, clothing and bric-a-brac. The nearest underground station is Old Street.

17

London's Food Markets

The Greater London area has scores of food markets, many of them farmers' markets which are run a few times a year. Many of them have websites and can be found by entering the words 'London food markets' followed by the name of the area which interests you in a search engine. There are far too many for them to be described in detail in the space available here so the following entries will be confined to a few which are of particular interest and in the central area.

Borough Market: from Chaucer to Art Deco

Borough Market, in Southwark, has a claim to be the oldest of all the capital's markets since its origins are lost in the early history of the capital. It claims to have existed by 1014 though the first reference to it in official documents occurs in 1276 during the reign of King Edward I, when it is recorded as having become a nuisance by spreading to the south side of London Bridge and thereby causing an obstruction to the heavy volumes of traffic crossing the river. Almost three centuries passed until the reign of Edward VI (1547–53) when the young king granted a charter which in 1550 vested the market rights in the Lord Mayor and citizens of the City who were thereby able to regulate the management of the market and the space which it occupied. The market sold grain, fruit, vegetables, fish and some livestock. In 1671 a new charter from Charles II fixed the limits of the market as extending from the southern end of London Bridge to St Margaret's Hill which lay close to the present site of Guy's Hospital and to the former home, in Talbot yard, of the Tabard Inn from which Chaucer's pilgrims set out for Canterbury.

By 1754 the continued chaos caused by traffic to and from the market prompted the City Corporation to petition parliament to relieve them of the responsibility of the market whose growth, in response to the increasing

This blue plaque in Talbot Yard marks the former site of the Tabard Inn, from which Chaucer's pilgrims set out in April, 1386. (Wikimedia Commons, BH2008)

population of London, had proved to be unmanageable. The Borough Market Act of 1756 therefore abolished the ancient market but gave the parish of St Saviour's Southwark (later Southwark Cathedral) the right to set up a market on a new site. A group of Southwark residents raised the money to purchase land in Rochester Yard, south of the Cathedral, occupying a smaller area than that of the 1671 market and equidistant between its limits. The present buildings were designed in 1851, with an Art Deco entrance from Southwark Street added in 1932, and in 2004 the south portico from Covent Garden's Floral Hall was installed when the Royal Opera House was redeveloped. By 1851 Borough Market had become one of London's most important. Its position close to the wharves of the Pool of London made it readily accessible to ships unloading their cargoes and it was well placed to supply retail and catering outlets both in the City and in the rapidly developing suburbs of South London.

Flying Leasehold

The market is situated beneath a railway junction whose tracks are the most heavily used in Great Britain, where trains from south of London, having passed through London Bridge Station, head for Cannon Street, Blackfriars,

Borough Market, underneath the busiest rail junction, with Southwark Cathedral in the background. (Wikimedia Commons, Josep Renailias)

Waterloo East and Charing Cross. This was a mixed blessing. On the one hand access to the railways meant that market traders had an additional source of produce from Kent and Sussex but on the other hand the market did not wish to give up any of its precious land for railway tracks and indeed was prevented from doing so by the terms of the 1756 Borough Market Act. An arrangement was made whereby the railway companies were granted a flying leasehold enabling them, from 1860, to build a viaduct carrying the permanent way while the market continued to trade beneath the arches. This arrangement continues and every time the railway viaduct is widened compensation is paid to the market trustees who number sixteen and who have to live in the area.

Over one hundred stallholders continue to sell fruit and vegetables, a blue plaque stating their claim to be the site of London's oldest market. To these have been added meat, fish and cheese and gourmet outlets such as De Gustibus breads, Furness Fish and Game and the Brindisa tapas restaurant amongst many others. The wholesale market operates on weekdays from 2 a.m. to 8 a.m. and the retail market on Thursdays, Fridays and Saturdays from 9 a.m. to 5 p.m., after which the area's restaurants and cafes continue to trade. In Shakespeare's time Southwark was the home of many theatres which were regarded as too louche to be accommodated within the City itself across London Bridge and the area was run down until the second half of the twentieth century. It then underwent a major revival with the South Bank developments, beginning with the Royal Festival Hall and the National Theatre. These were followed in 1997 by the opening of Shakespeare's Globe, within walking distance of the market along the riverbank. The original Globe was destroyed by fire in 1613 and the present theatre, inspired by the American actor Sam Wanamaker, is as faithful a reproduction of the original as fire regulations will permit. Three years later the Tate Modern art gallery was opened in the converted Bankside power station so the South Bank, from being a poor relation of the City, has become its cultural neighbour. Many visitors combine a visit to the bustling Borough Market with a visit to the Globe or the gallery followed by a meal at one of the many restaurants which are found in the vicinity of the market.

The Southbank Real Food Market

A short distance upstream, on the Southbank Centre Square, behind the Royal Festival Hall, the Real Food Market is held every weekend from Friday to Sunday. It offers a range of food and drink sold by those who make it. Grass-fed beef and free-range chicken straight from the farm are for sale together with fresh fish caught the day it is sold. Farmhouse cheeses, locally baked bread, hand-roasted coffee, bread, charcuterie and wine from Spain, Italy and France are found alongside seasonal fruit and vegetables, cakes and desserts and beers from small-scale producers. By taking the riverside path Queen's Walk to reach the food market the visitor will pass through the Southbank Centre's book market. Sheltered as it is beneath Waterloo Bridge it is one of the very few open-air book markets that is held every day with a selection of second-hand and rare books to meet the most eclectic tastes.

Chapel Market

Islington's Chapel market, on a street of that name north of the Angel and west of Islington High Street is known only to a few aficionados but has a place in sporting as well as trading history. It sells fruit, vegetables and fish as well as low-cost household goods and clothing. It is open every day except Monday and now accommodates London's first farmer's market on Sundays at the west end, adjacent to Penton Street. Also at the Penton Street end is a gastro pub with a unique name, A Hundred Crows Rising, while at the opposite, eastern, end is a pub called The Agricultural. This is a reference to the fact that Upper Street, a continuation of Islington High Street, was a route for cattle which were being driven to market at Smithfield. Chapel Market is also the home of Manze's Pie,

Eel and Mash Shop which has been selling this traditional Cockney food for over a century. A short walk away, in Islington High Street outside the entrance to Angel underground station, is a covered antiques market.

In the midst of Chapel market, running a short distance from its north side, is White Conduit Street which in the eighteenth century briefly flourished as a spa. The surrounding fields were much favoured by the aristocracy for games of cricket who formed the White Conduit Club on the site. However, since the fields were a public space the earls, honourables and colonels had to share them with more plebeian players so they asked one of their bowlers who had experience in the purchase and sale of property to acquire some ground where they could play in private. This he duly did in Dorset Square, close to the present site of Marylebone Station but when a fellow business-man offered him a good price for it he sold out and purchased a larger site in the less fashionable vicinity of St John's Wood. He gave his own name to the cricket ground. He was Thomas Lord.

Berwick Street Market

Berwick Street, in the heart of Soho, was built in the late seventeenth century. It was created by the Duke of Berwick, an illegitimate son of the Catholic James II, and the duke may have built the street to protect the owner of the land, James Pollett, who was himself a Roman Catholic. It was described in 1720, not long after it was completed, by John Strype in his updated version of John Stow's *Survey of London* in flattering terms, 'a pretty handsome, straight street, with new, well-built houses much inhabited by the French where they have a church'. 'The French' were the Huguenot population of Soho which had grown rapidly as a result of the persecutions of Louis XIV of France. The handsome buildings remain, though the church has gone; it was originally one of many Huguenot churches in the area of which one remains in nearby Soho Square.

The market, selling mainly fruit and vegetables, is as old as the street and is open from Monday to Saturday. There are also many shops selling unusual cloths, some of them attended by burly doormen who appear to be there to act as 'minders'. The market has been joined by an impressive collection of delicatessens and wine merchants and has become the centre of Soho's trade in food of all kinds. The street also has more colourful residents including record-ing studios, advertising agencies and was for long the home of the Raymond Revue Bar which, by becoming a club, was able to stage nude shows. The area is also well supplied with cafes and restaurants of every kind. The lower part of Berwick Street is for pedestrians and leads, through Walker's Court, to Rupert Street whose street market is effectively an extension of Berwick Street's, though mostly devoted to clothing, CDs and London memorabilia.

18

Portobello Road Antiques Market

A War Over An Ear

Portobello Road, in Notting Hill, owes its name to an incident in the War of Jenkins' Ear, a conflict with Spain which began in 1739 following the alleged removal of the ear of Robert Jenkins, captain of a merchant ship, by a Spanish crew. The severed ear was duly exhibited to an indignant parliament though some doubts remained about the precise character of the incident. In 1739 the port of Porto Bello, in what is now Panama, was captured by Admiral Vernon and in a display of patriotic fervour a new farm was built in the vicinity of the present Exmoor Street, to the west of Portobello Road. It was given the name Portobello Farm in place of the original, more prosaic, Green's Lane, a path leading from Kensington to Kensal Green. In the reign of Victoria, Portobello Road, linking the farm at its northern end with Kensington and Notting Hill to the south, was turned from fields and orchards to dwellings and the road is still characterised by fine Victorian terraces. George Orwell lived at No. 22, Portobello Road when he returned from service in the Imperial Police in Burma in 1927. Something of the atmosphere of the street at that time is conveyed by the experience of Orwell and his landlord and landlady Mr and Mrs Craig when they inadvertently locked themselves out of the house one evening. Orwell suggested that they ask the neighbours if they could borrow their ladder to gain entry. Mrs Craig declined. Having lived next to them for fourteen years and not spoken to them she saw no reason to start in such circumstances. They all walked a mile in the dark to borrow a ladder from a relative. Nearby was the more sinister Rillington Place where John Christie murdered at least eight women. It was renamed Ruston Close which was in turn demolished to make way for Westway though Ruston Mews, nearby, remains. The area was at one time rundown. It was touched by the race riots which disfigured the area in 1958 when the arrival of Afro-Caribbean immigrants to the area to occupy property owned by the infamous Peter Rachman

George Orwell's lodgings in Portobello Road. (Wikimedia Commons, Alexrk2)

provoked violence between the immigrants and white youths lasting for a week in August and September of that year. The following year the Notting Hill Carnival began as a response to the interracial tension and has since become Europe's biggest street carnival.

Peter Rachman (1919–62)

Rachman was a Polish immigrant of Jewish descent who, after escaping from both the invading Nazis and a Soviet labour camp, fought with the Allies and settled in London after the war. In the 1950s he acquired a number of mansion blocks in what was then the run-down area of Notting Hill and rented them out to Afro-Caribbean immigrants who were having difficulty in finding accommodation elsewhere. He was accused of using devious tactics to remove existing (mostly white) tenants whose rents were controlled and replacing them with multi-occupancy immigrants who enjoyed no such protection. The term Rachmanism was introduced to describe such practices. More recent accounts of his life have cast doubt upon his alleged ruthlessness. After his death he acquired a degree of notoriety because of a distant connection with the Profumo affair when it emerged that Christine Keeler, who had had a brief affair with the Minister of War John Profumo, had also been the mistress of Peter Rachman. The area in which Peter Rachman's property empire flourished has been redeveloped and is one of London's most expensive residential districts.

Portobello Road is almost 2 miles in length and on Saturdays much of it, from Golborne Road to Westbourne Grove, is the home of Britain's largest and most celebrated antiques market. A fresh food market was created in the Victorian era as the area became residential, with a few dealers in curios and antiques but the antique dealers, who arrived in force after the Second World War, now predominate. Some of them trade from shops but on Saturday mornings stallholders fill the street. If there is any order in the way in which the stalls are

Portobello Road. (Arpingstone, public domain)

arranged this writer has failed to detect it. Those seeking a bargain are best advised to visit the event with a clear idea of what is sought, having researched the subject beforehand and avoid the temptations presented by other merchandise. Bargaining is to be expected. The road is also home, at No. 191 Portobello Road, to the Electric Cinema one of Britain's oldest cinemas, opened in 1911, in a Grade II listed building and each August the road hosts a film festival. The cinema was refurbished in 2001 to a level of luxury which offers its patrons leather armchairs, footstools, tables and food service.

Arthur Daley, Del Trotter and Friends

The market has given its name to its own board game, 'Portobello Road' and has frequently featured in literature, television and in films. Portobello Road was the scene of a car chase in the 1950 Ealing studios film *The Blue Lamp* starring Dirk Bogarde and Jack Warner and was also a backdrop in the 1971 musical *Bedknobs and Broomsticks* while Paddington Bear, the creation of Michael Bond, visited Portobello Market each day. From Monday to Friday he would find more vegetables than antiques on sale but he drank coffee with his friend Mr Gruber in the latter's antiques shop at 11 o'clock each morning. The street was often visited by Arthur Daley in the cult TV series *Minder* in the 1970s and Arthur's favourite haunt, the Winchester Club is presumably somewhere in the area. In the twenty-first century the market is often visited by contestants in the antiques-based game show *Bargain Hunt*. Ruth Rendell's 2008 novel *Portobello* is set in the area, as was one of Muriel Spark's short stories *Portobello Road*. However, the prize for the best-known fictional use of the area is contested between two works. The first is an episode of *Only Fools and Horses* in which Del and Rodney Trotter purchase a statue of Kubera from a dealer in Portobello Road. The other contender is the film *Notting Hill* in which bookshop-owner Will Thacker (Hugh Grant) is visited by film star Anna Scott (Julia Roberts) in search of a title at Will's travel bookshop at No. 161, Portobello Road. When Will later meets Anna in the street and inadvertently spills orange juice on her clothes he invites her to change at his flat, nearby, behind a blue door. The door belonged to a house at No. 280, Westbourne Park Road, the home of Richard Curtis who wrote the screenplay for *Notting Hill* (as well as *Four Weddings and a Funeral* and *Blackadder*. The door, now famous, was auctioned for charity and replaced by a black one. Much of the filming for *Notting Hill* took place on Portobello Road.

The most convenient underground stations for Portobello Road are Notting Hill Gate and Ladbroke Grove.

19

Camden Markets: Not One But Six

Note the plural *markets*. The institution frequently referred to as Camden Market is not one but six different markets occupying a large area near the Regent's Canal where it passes through Camden Town on its way to the Thames. All the markets are at their busiest at weekends, especially Sundays, though some activity is to be found on weekdays. The first is Camden Lock Market, a name that is sometimes applied to the whole complex, close to Camden Town Station on the Northern Line. The site was originally occupied by warehouses and other premises belonging to the Grand Union Canal Company whose freight traffic virtually ended after the big freeze of the winter of 1962–63. The market consists mostly of stalls selling craft products, clothing and bric-a-brac and is open on Saturdays and Sundays, the latter being the busiest day when scores of thousands of visitors are to be expected. Indeed it owes it origins to the fact that, prior to the Sunday Trading Act of 1994, supermarkets were not allowed to open on Sundays. A three-storey market hall was added to the market in the 1990s. Inverness Street Market, nearby, was once a thriving market for fresh produce but competition from supermarkets has reduced it to a handful of stalls selling fruit and vegetables. A feature of the area, adjoining the canal, is Camden Lock Studios in the former home of the short-lived *TV-AM*, launched in February 1983 as a high-minded 'Mission to explain' to the British public over its cornflakes. The British public opted instead for Roland Rat and in 1991 the franchise was awarded to another broadcaster. The studio, with its distinctive 'eggcups' on the roof was sold and plans are in hand for it to be redeveloped.

Almost adjacent to Camden Lock Market is the Stables Market which occupies what were once the stables and horse hospital belonging to Pickford's and date from the time that Pickford's conveyed most of its consignments by canal. Many of the market's stalls and shops are sheltered by railway arches and a market hall was added in 2006. Some are in the horse tunnels which were used for taking horse-drawn merchandise beneath what is now the West Coast Main Line out of Euston Station. Clothing is a feature of the Stables Market, with several traders specialising in black clothing for 'goths' and 'cybergoths'. It is also the main centre for the sale of furniture within the complex of markets. Chain stores are not admitted, a feature of the market which has been fiercely defended by market traders and local residents. Stalls occasionally attract celebrity occupants such as the disc jockey Chris Evans who was briefly a stallholder in December 2004.

Camden Lock Village Market, to the east of Chalk Farm Road, runs along the canal towpath and was severely damaged in a fire of 2008. It reopened in 2009 and, besides the clothing which is found throughout the Camden markets, it also has a number of more unusual traders including one who specialises in percussion instruments and a glass engraver. The Buck Street Market, which is a few yards north of Camden Town Station, consists mostly of clothing, some of them designed by the stallholders themselves. Finally The Electric Ballroom is a nightclub which, at weekends during the daytime, functions as an indoor market for independent designers.

The markets attract over twenty million visitors a year and at weekends this imposes severe strains on the underground stations, especially Camden Town. Kentish Town and Mornington Crescent stations are also a short walk from the markets.

20

London's Lost Markets

Many of London's markets are lost but not entirely forgotten. They survive only in the names of streets, buildings or, in one case, simply a commemorative plaque. Others have been absorbed by their more prosperous brethren. Some are described in the pages that follow.

The Corn Exchange

One of the most important markets in mediaeval London was the Corn Market. London's first public granary gave its name in 1438 to the street in which it was established, Cornhill. Wheat, barley and rye were landed at Billingsgate and Queenhithe and taken by cart to warehouses and markets at Cornhill and also Cheapside, off which ran Bread Street, home to the City's bakers. As the City grew, the quantities of corn were such that it was no longer convenient to cart the produce through the congested streets so a Metropolitan Corn Market was established at Bear Quay off Lower Thames Street where the Custom House now stands. The name Bear Quay is believed to refer to the quantities of barley that were landed there for brewing beer at the City's many breweries. Strype referred to it as, 'The great corn market by Billingsgate'. In 1747 a Corn Exchange was built nearby, between Mark Lane and Seething Lane, where traders could strike bargains. The building was extended in the nineteenth century, destroyed by bombing in 1941, reopened in 1954 and replaced by a new building in 1973 in Seething Lane. Cereals of every kind, pulse vegetables, flour, seeds, animal feeds and fertilisers were traded there until 1987 when the market moved to the floor of the Baltic Exchange. The building on Seething Lane remains, now an office.

The Coal Exchange

A more controversial loss was that of the Coal Exchange, also in Lower Thames Street. It was on the north side of the street, almost opposite the old Billingsgate fish market. Originally opened in 1770 it was replaced in 1849 by the City architect J.B. Bunning, who also rebuilt Billingsgate and it was one of London's first buildings constructed with a cast-iron frame, shortly before the more famous Crystal Palace was erected in 1851 for the Great Exhibition, using the same material on a much greater scale. When it was built the excavation work for its foundations found an elaborate Roman hypocaust, one of the first examples of this early central heating system found in Britain. The market was a fine example of early Victorian architecture, with a wooden floor inlaid with a representation of a compass. Four floors of offices were surmounted by a fine dome and the entrance was marked by a tower topped by a rotunda. The dome was decorated with panels relating to the coal trade, depicting fossils of ferns and palms, images of coal mines and views of Newcastle, Durham, Sunderland and North Shields from where the coal came. The building was opened by Prince Albert on 30 October 1849, the ceremony being marked by the fact that it was the last time the royal barge was used for such a purpose.

At the time London was heated and powered almost entirely by coal, with more than 3 million tons being brought by sea and river from Northumberland and Durham. The trade, using about 3,000 vessels, has left its mark on London in other ways, notably in the popular Wapping pub The Prospect of Whitby, named after a vessel from that Northumberland port. Duties on coal, known as metage, were collected by the City Corporation and paid for much of the reconstruction of London after the Great Fire of 1666. The duties covered the costs of rebuilding St Paul's Cathedral and, in the nineteenth century, they paid for the Victoria Embankment between Westminster Bridge and Blackfriars Bridge. As the century progressed the importation of coal to London increased though a growing proportion was carried by rail. The exchange continued to prosper and did so until the coal industry was nationalised in 1947.

The building was damaged by bombing during the Second World War and, although it was used as an office after its use as a coal exchange ceased, it languished and fell into a poor condition. In 1958 it became a Grade II listed building but it stood in the way of the City's plans to carry out a much-needed widening of Lower Thames Street. As the prospect of its demolition loomed, the great and the good of architecture and conservation rallied to its defence. They included the architectural historian Nikolaus Pevsner; the founder of the Bauhaus, Walter Gropius; and, most vociferous of all, John Betjeman. Despite their efforts the building was demolished in 1962 and its only surviving

The Coal Exchange, 1808. (Wikimedia Commons)

artefacts are two cast-iron dragons, which were salvaged from the para-pet above the entrance and re-erected in Temple Gardens off the Victoria Embankment to mark the boundary between the City and Westminster.

Plantation House

Reference has been made elsewhere (see page 75) to the Mincing Lane Tea and Rubber Brokers' Association, set up in 1909 to deal in those commodi-ties whose volatility in price made them unattractive to many traders. In 1935 Plantation House was built to provide a home for a number of such markets. It was for many years the centre of the world's trade in tea and in 1954 it became the home of the London Commodity Exchange where futures in cocoa, coffee, grain, potatoes, rice and soya beans were traded. In 1987 the exchange moved to St Katherine's Dock in London's docklands as London Fox (Futures and Options Exchange) before being absorbed by LIFFE (see page 102) in 1996. Plantation House survived until 2004 when it was replaced by Plantation Place at No. 30, Fenchurch Street, which now provides offices for insurance companies and consultancies. Plantation House was long the recognised centre of the world's tea and rubber trade, the latter having now moved to Barking, but it also accommodated many other markets. The London Cocoa Terminal Market was founded in 1928 and moved into Plantation

House. It is now conducted mainly by computerised trading in which dealers offer spot prices for those who wish to buy and sell immediately; and futures contracts for those for whom cocoa is an essential raw material, such as confectionery companies, and who wish to secure a guaranteed price in the medium term free of anxieties associated with the harvest. The business is conducted mainly in London and New York. Plantation House was also for many years the home of the London Sugar Association which was founded in 1882 to provide rules under which raw sugar was traded. It is now based in an office at No. 154, Bishopsgate. It was also, for a short time, the home of the London Metals Exchange (see separate entry on page 108).

Hungerford Market

Hungerford Market, which has no connection with the Berkshire town of that name, is now remembered only by the railway bridge into Charing Cross Station and the accompanying footbridge across the Thames. The site, now occupied by the station, was purchased by Sir Walter Hungerford from Farleigh Hungerford Castle, near Bath, in 1425. Sir Walter was the Speaker of the House of Commons and built his home on the site. The family's fortunes fluctuated as royal dynasties came and went with one member being hanged at Tyburn for murder in 1523 and another being executed on the order of Henry VIII because of his association with the discredited Thomas Cromwell and because he had supposedly tried to shorten the king's life by casting a spell. Adultery, attempts to poison spouses and spells in prison also marked the family's passage through several generations. They were a colourful lot! The property was finally restored to Sir Edward Hungerford (1632–1711) by Charles II and it was Sir Edward who obtained permission to hold a market there three days a week, explaining that his house on the site was 'so old and ruinous that the same could not be rebuilt without great expense'. The market, which opened in 1682, consisted of shops and a covered piazza, but did not prosper under the management of the family and shares in it were sold to a number of investors. One of these was Christopher Wren who probably designed the small market house in the centre of the site. In 1718 the market was bought by Henry Wise, a nurseryman and superintendent of the royal gardens and was sold by his family to the newly-formed Hungerford Market Company in 1830.

A Fresh Start

In 1831 a fine new market in granite was built on the site, designed by Charles Fowler, architect of Covent Garden, and built by Samuel Morton Peto who

Hungerford Market, 1850, viewed from the original footbridge. The market site is now occupied by Charing Cross station. (Wikimedia Commons)

also built Nelson's Column (before going bankrupt). It was an ambitious project, with a wharf on the river and the market itself stretching up to the present site of Trafalgar Square. The new London Bridge, designed by John Rennie and opened in 1831, made it much easier for fishing vessels to gain access to the upper reaches of the Thames than had been the case with the narrow-arched mediaeval bridge so adjacent to the Hungerdord wharf was a fish market which, it was hoped, would provide competition for Billingsgate in supplying fresh fish to the West End. This was itself expanding rapidly at the time with the construction of Belgravia and Pimlico on land which had previously been a swamp. A flight of steps led from the fish market to a timber-roofed fruit and vegetable market and this, in turn, to a meat market which could be reached from the Strand. No effort was spared to make the market a success. Its opening in July 1833 offered flights in a balloon, and a steamboat service brought customers to the market from as far afield as Woolwich and Vauxhall. A suspension bridge designed by Isambard Kingdom Brunel close to the site of the present Hungerford footbridge gave access to Lambeth from 1845 and in 1851 London's first ice-cream stall was opened in the market by the Swiss-Italian Carlo Gatti. In the same year Hungerford Hall was added to the site to take advantage of the crowds visiting the Great Exhibition in Hyde Park, with lecturers and conjurers providing a wide variety of entertainment.

The market was praised by contemporary writers for its butter and for its meat and fruit pies.

Despite the best efforts of the company the market failed to prosper in competition with Billingsgate, Smithfield and Covent Garden and was damaged by fire in 1854. In 1862 the South-Eastern Railway, which was seeking a site for a London terminus north of the Thames, offered to purchase the site which duly became the home of Charing Cross railway station, opening in 1864. Brunel's bridge was dismantled and replaced by the present railway bridge, the chains from the suspension bridge being used in the construction of Clifton suspension bridge, also designed by Brunel though built after his death in 1859.

Clare Market

This forgotten market is now the home of the London School of Economics one of whose directors, Ralf Dahrendorf, adopted the title Baron Dahrendorf of Clare Market when he became a life peer in 1993. It lies to the north of the Aldwych, off Kingsway and owes its origins to its former owner, the Earl of Clare, who constructed a small market hall there in the 1650s not far from

The London School of Economics now occupies the site of the former tripe houses of Clare Market. (Wikimedia Commons, Umezo KAMATA)

his home off the Strand. The small market hall was surrounded by butchers and grocers, with butchers predominating, including an area set aside for kosher butchers. In 1850 it was estimated that there were about twenty-six butchers who slaughtered as many as 400 sheep and 200 bullocks each week, with consequences for local sanitation that may scarcely be imagined. A tripe house boiled the offal nearby. The son of Charles Dickens, also Charles, left an account of the market after a visit in 1879 in which he recorded that London's poorest were to be found frequenting the market on a Saturday evening, its shops 'filled with strange pieces of coarse, dark-coloured and unwholesome-looking meat'. The seventeenth-century buildings, which escaped the Great Fire, survived until the twentieth century to become one of London's worst slums. The site was redeveloped by the London County Council to create the Aldwych and Kingsway after 1900 and in the 1920s it became the home of the London School of Economics which had been founded in 1895. One of its main buildings takes its name from the market.

The Steelyard: The First Common Market?

In 2005 a plaque was placed at Cannon Street Station to mark the former location of the London trading post of one of Europe's most extraordinary phenomena: the Hanseatic League, or Hansa. In 1259 five cities in what is now Germany, Lubeck, Hamburg, Cologne, Rostock and Wismar formed a league, soon called the Hansa ('trading guild') which was a trading bloc, free of taxes, designed to cooperate in the sale of herrings from the Baltic. By 1400 the league had been joined by cities as far as Novgorod, Riga and Krakov in what later became Russia, Latvia and Poland and it had its own fleet defending its merchants in the North Sea and the Baltic. It was, in effect, a confederation of European cities, an early common market, trading freely with one another in a wide variety of commodities regardless of national boundaries. In the west it created a number of trading posts. One of these was in King's Lynn, where the Hanseatic warehouse still survives as the local register office but the most important was in London and was known as the Steelyard. The origin of the name is unclear and may refer to a mechanism of that name which was used for weighing sacks of grain. An alternative meaning is simply 'market stall' in an old German dialect.

Pawning the Crown Jewels

According to John Stow, 'Merchants of Almaine' (German merchants) had been trading in London since 1259, the year the confederation was first formed since in that year King Henry III granted those, 'having a house in

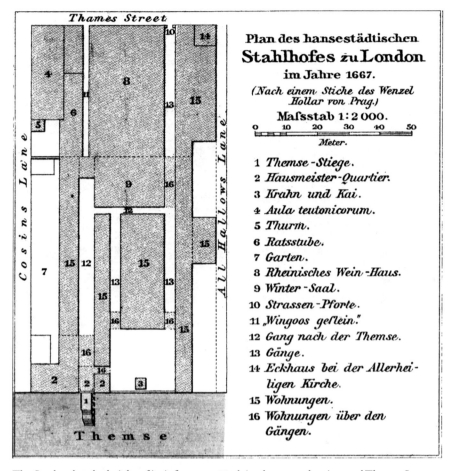

Plan des hansestädtischen

Stahlhofes zu London

im Jahre 1667.

(Nach einem Stiche des Wenzel Hollar von Prag.)

Mafsstab 1 : 2 000.

Meter.

1 *Themse-Stiege.*
2 *Hausmeister-Quartier.*
3 *Krahn und Kai.*
4 *Aula teutonicorum.*
5 *Thurm.*
6 *Ratsstube.*
7 *Garten.*
8 *Rheinisches Wein-Haus.*
9 *Winter-Saal.*
10 *Strassen-Pforte.*
11 *„Wingoos geflein."*
12 *Gang nach der Themse.*
13 *Gänge.*
14 *Eckhaus bei der Allerheiligen Kirche.*
15 *Wohnungen.*
16 *Wohnungen über den Gängen.*

The Steelyard at the height of its influence, 1667, lying between the river and Thames Street, a site now occupied by the trains of Cannon Street station. All that now remains of it is a passage linking Cousin Lane and Allhallows Lane beneath Cannon Street station. (Wikimedia Commons, Droysen/Andrée)

the City of London' the right to enjoy 'such freedoms and liberties as by the king and his noble progenitors they had and enjoyed'. If Stow's dates were correct (which is by no means certain) then German merchants were trading in London well before the league itself was formed. The Hanseatic merchants who created the Steelyard later in the century gained a number of privileges from successive monarchs in return for financial support. In 1339 Edward III pawned the crown jewels to Hanseatic merchants from Cologne in return for a loan to finance the early stages of the Hundred Years' War with France and they were also given concessions in the trading of Cornish tin and the export of English wool. Hanseatic merchants also assumed responsibility for the repair of Bishopsgate. In 1381 the Steelyard was wrecked by followers of

This plaque, by the riverside footpath to the east of Cannon Street station, commemorates the Hanseatic "Steelyard" of medieval London. (Wikimedia Commons, Ian Mansfield)

Wat Tyler during the Peasants' Revolt and in 1492 it was besieged by London merchants who resented the fact that the Steelyard had something approaching a monopoly of wool exports. By this time the Steelyard contained its own church, weighing house (hence probably the name 'steelyard'), offices and residences, with its own wharf on the banks of the Thames.

Sir Thomas Gresham, having founded the Royal Exchange, persuaded Elizabeth I that the Steelyard's privileges were excessive: not only did they have a substantial share of English exports, especially in wool, they also refused to use English ships. Elizabeth removed the advantages enjoyed by the Hansa but German merchants continued to occupy the Steelyard's premises which became known as the Rhenish Garden. It served wines and beer from Germany in the open air, one of its more appreciative and regular customers being Samuel Pepys who made several references to it in his diary. In 1853 the site was sold to the South Eastern Railway as a site for its City terminus which opened in 1866, two years after its west end terminus at Charing Cross on the former site of Hungerford Market. The location of the Steelyard was unmarked for 139 years until the plaque was placed at Cannon Street Station in 2005.

Shepherd Market

Shepherd Market, in the heart of Mayfair, has one of the most exclusive collections of boutiques and restaurants in the capital. James II established the fifteen-day May Fair in the 1680s mainly for cattle trading but as the area was developed for grand houses in the eighteenth century its rowdiness and the waste which accompanied the market made it an unruly neighbour for its aristocratic residents and the fair was closed. Mayfair is now best known as the occupant of the last and most expensive space on the board game 'Monopoly'. The fair moved out (to Haymarket) and a local architect, Edward Shepherd, was invited to develop the area in 1735. Over the next decade he created a small paved market square with a duck pond, a small theatre and narrow surrounding alleys which now accommodate an eclectic mix of old pubs, restaurants, clothing shops and a hardware shop. They include a restaurant serving classic French cuisine L'Artiste Muscle; a Polish-Mexican bistro (surely a unique combination) called L'Autre; and another French restaurant Le Boudin Blanc (literally translated as 'white black pudding'; a speciality of the house). Many will remember Tiddy Dol's restaurant, at No. 55 Shepherd Market, serving classic English food like steak and kidney pudding and named

England's last surviving Hanseatic warehouse at King's Lynn, Norfolk, now the home of the registry office. (Wikimedia Commons)

after Tiddy Dol the gingerbread maker who used to ply his trade at Tyburn during executions. The restaurant closed in 1998.

The novelist Michael Arlen rented rooms opposite the public house The Grapes and set his 1924 novel *The Green Hat* in the market. In the eighteenth century James Boswell lived nearby. The area is also frequently encountered in fiction, with the residences of characters in the fiction of Evelyn Waugh joined by Bertie Wooster and Jeeves who lived nearby in Half Moon Street. It has also long been known for its population of prostitutes, where the peer and novelist Jeffrey Archer encountered Monica Coghlan which led to his downfall when he was gaoled for perjury over his relationship with her.

Postscript

This account of London's markets has included a small selection of the hundreds of markets which are to be found in the Greater London area. A website, www.londonmarkets.co.uk, contains a fuller list divided into areas: North, South, East, West and Central London, with basic details of each market. If you wish to find markets in your area, or which specialise in merchandise of special interest to you, then that is a good place to start.

Good hunting!

Chronology

c. **600 BC:** Thales created the first options contract

AD 79: Roman Forum, close to Leadenhall Market, became Roman London's trading centre

878: Alfred the Great granted the defeated Danes the right to trade at Aldwych 'Old Market'

1014: Borough Market, London's oldest, opened in Southwark

1133: Charter granted for Bartholomew Fair

1174: First recorded horse race in England took place at Smithfield

1197: Hospital of St Mary Spittal founded; later known as Spitalfields

1200: A convent Garden created by Westminster Abbey, north of Strand, later called 'Covent Garden'

13th Century: 'Steelyard' created by German Hanseatic merchants on north bank of the Thames

1209: London Bridge rebuilt in stone, surmounted by houses and shops; bridge survived until 1831

1282: Stocks fruit and vegetable market established on present site of Mansion House

1296: First documentary reference to market at 'Leaden Hall'

1305: William Wallace executed at Smithfield

1381: Wat Tyler killed at Smithfield, ending Peasants' Revolt

1488: Navigation Acts: English merchants obliged to use English ships

1555: Queen Mary I granted charter to Muscovy Company

1570: First Royal Exchange opened by Queen Elizabeth I

1583: World's first life insurance policy taken out at Royal Exchange on William Gibbons, salter

1600: East India Company granted charter by Queen Elizabeth I

1603: John Stow's *Survey of London* published

1638: Inigo Jones completed Covent Garden piazza and St Paul's church Charles I granted a licence for sale of flesh, poultry and vegetables at Spitalfields

1652: London's first coffee stall opened on St Michael's Alley, Cornhill

1666: The Great Fire of London; burned itself out at Pye Corner, Smithfield

1669: Garraway's Coffee House opened in Exchange Alley (now Change Alley)

1670: Covent Garden Market received charter from Charles II

Late 17th Century: Huguenot refugees arrived in England, fleeing persecution by Louis XIV

1682: Hungerford Market opened

c. **1688:** Edward Lloyd opened coffee house in Tower Street; moved to Lombard Street, 1691

1694: Bank of England founded

1696: 'Lloyd's News' first published, later renamed 'Lloyd's list'

1698: Dealers in stocks banned from Royal Exchange for 'loitering and gambling'

1720: South Sea Bubble

1739: Porto Bello farm created

1744: Virginia and Baltic Coffee House: first home of Baltic exchange

1755: Dr Johnson's *Dictionary* described a jobber as 'a low wretch'

1756: Borough Market Act

1762: Barings bank founded

1770: Coal Exchange opened in Lower Thames Street

1774: Lloyd's moved to Royal Exchange

1801: New Stock Exchange building in Capel Court, east of Bank of England

1814: Thomas Cochrane, naval hero, fined for rigging the stock market with false rumours

1830: Liverpool to Manchester Railway opened

Covent Garden Market rebuilt by Charles Fowler

Hogge Lane became Middlesex Street, the site of Petticoat Lane Market

1833: New Hungerford Market opened

1839: Navigation Acts repealed: free trade rules

1844: The new Royal Exchange opened by Queen Victoria

1845: Julius Reuter used pigeons and later telegraphs to transmit market news

1846: Railway mania; prices started to collapse

1848: Last great Chartist demonstration caused stock market anxieties: passed off peacefully

1851: submarine cable to France (and New York, 1866); market information available in minutes

Present Borough Market Buildings constructed;

1855: Metropolitan Cattle Market opened at Copenhagen Fields to replace Smithfield

1857: Baltic Company purchased South Sea House

1858: Lutine Bell installed at Lloyd's

1860: Joseph Malin opened Britain's first fish and chip shop in Whitechapel

Flying leasehold granted to enable railway viaduct to run above Borough Market

1862: Hungerford Market demolished to make way for Charing Cross station

1866: Cannon Street station opened on site of former Steelyard

1868: Smithfield Meat Market opened, designed by Sir Horace Jones

Foreign & Colonial Investment Trust launched

1869: Columbia Road flower market opened, paid for by Angela Burdett-Coutts

1876: Robert Horner built the first Spitalfields market hall: the present structure

1877: Billingsgate Fish Market rebuilt by Sir Horace Jones

London Metal Exchange founded

1880: First consignment of refrigerated meat arrived from Australia and New Zealand

1881: New Leadenhall Market opened; designed by Sir Horace Jones

1886: Gold discovered on the Witwatersrand, South Africa

1903: Baltic Exchange moved to St Mary Axe

1904: Lloyd's wrote the first car policy

1911: Lloyd's wrote first aviation policy

1923: Stock Exchange adopted it motto 'Dictum Meum Pactum' – 'My Word is My Bond'

1927: George Orwell moved to No. 22, Portobello Road

1929: October: Wall Street Crash: markets and economies in turmoil

1934: Keynes's 'General Theory' published, proposing government intervention in failing economies

1942: Stock Exchange allowed two women to be employed as clerks

1944: Bretton Woods system agreed for managing international trade and finance

1950: New Caledonian Market opened in Bermondsey: London's last *Marché Ouvert*

1954: 4 July; Rationing ended and event celebrated at Smithfield as meat came off the ration

1962: Covent Garden Market purchased by Greater London Council
Coal Exchange demolished to make way for road widening

1966: George Cornell shot dead in the Blind Beggar pub by Ronnie Kray

1969: Cromer Report proposed recruitment of more Lloyd's 'names'

1972: Stock Exchange moved from Capel Court to Throgmorton Street

1973: Women admitted to full membership of London Stock Exchange

1974: Covent Garden fruit and vegetable wholesale market relocated to Nine Elms, Lambeth

1982: LIFFE (London International Financial Futures Exchange) opened in Royal Exchange
Billingsgate moved to its new site in Docklands

1984: Minimum commission system abolished on Stock exchange
British Telecom first major privatisation, followed by many others in UK and abroad

1986: 'Big Bang' transformed trading on the Stock Exchange
New Lloyd's building opened designed by Richard Rogers

1987: BP privatisation proceeded despite collapse of stock market prices in October's 'Big Crash'

1988: Lloyd's announced largest ever loss of £510 million; beginning of 'asbestos', etc. troubles

1992: Baltic Exchange destroyed by IRA bomb
September: 'Black Wednesday' and pound left European ERM

1995: Baltic Exchange moved to new premises at No. 38, St Mary Axe
Barings Bank collapsed

1996: Lutine Bell rung an unprecedented three times to mark end of Lloyd's crisis

1997: Shakespeare's Globe opened on South Bank, near Borough Market

2004: Stock exchange moved to Paternoster Square

2005: Plaque at Cannon Street station to mark former site of Steelyard

2007: Northern Rock collapsed and start of financial meltdown for some banks

2014: Borough Market celebrates its 1,000th anniversary

From 221B Baker Street to the Old Curiosity Shop

Stephen Halliday

9780752470245

London is unrivalled as a source of inspiration for writers, from Geoffrey Chaucer to J.K. Rowling. All of London's clubs, pubs, restaurants, houses and streets that have been made famous in the works of the likes of Sir Arthur Conan Doyle, Ian Fleming and Charles Dickens are featured in this volume.

Underground to Everywhere

Stephen Halliday

9780752497723

London's Underground is one of the best-known and most distinctive aspects of the city. Stephen Halliday's wide-ranging history of the Underground celebrates the vision and determination of the Victorian Pioneers who conceived this revolutionary transport system. His book records the scandal, disappointments, and disasters that have punctuated the story and the careers of those that have shaped its history.

The Little Book of London

David Long

9780750948005

The Little Book of London is a funny, fast-paced, fact-packed compendium full of the sort of frivolous, fantastic or simply strange information which no one will want to be without. Containing London's looniest laws, its most eccentric inhabitants, the realities of being royal and literally hundreds of wacky facts about the world's greatest city.

Visit our website and discover thousands of other History Press books.
www.thehistorypress.co.uk